WELCOME TO CANADIAN ENGLISH

A BASIC HANDBOOK FOR STUDENTS LIVING IN ONTARIO PART I

AUTHORS: LILLIAN BUTOVSKY / ESTHER PODOLIAK

The Ontario Ministry of Citizenship and Culture

Susan Fish, Minister

Credits

Assistance with editing, writing and
co-ordinating: John McHugh
Illustrations: Ken Gray, Advertising
Design: H. Bruce Dorland & Assoc.
Stamps on page 112 reproduced courtesy
of Canada Post Corporation.

Published by the
Ministry of Citizenship and Culture.
Printed by the Queen's Printer
for Ontario
Province of Ontario
Toronto, Canada

© 1984 Government of Ontario

Copies available at $2.00 from the
Ontario Government Bookstore,
880 Bay St., Toronto
for personal shopping.
Out-of-town customers write to
Publications Services Section,
5th Floor, 880 Bay St., Toronto, Ontario,
M7A 1N8. Telephone 965-6015.
Toll free long distance 1-800-268-7540;
in Northwestern Ontario 0-Zenith 67200.

D1476 11/84 20M
ISBN-0-7743-9384-X

CONTENTS

UNIT 1: SELF-INTRODUCTIONS

CONVERSATION: Tony Meets Ana

Ana

Tony

First, look at ALL the pictures. Then look at EACH picture.
WHAT IS THE PERSON SAYING? TRY TO GUESS.

1

2

3

4

5

6

WORDS FOR THE CONVERSATION

1

Hello.

2

I'm Tony.

3

I'm Ana.

4

Nice to meet you.

5

Where are you from?

6

Chile.

Other Sentences You May Hear

You can say the same thing in more than one way. For example, in Picture 1, Tony can say "Hi" instead of "Hello." Here are some other examples.

Picture 2: My name is Tony.
Picture 3: My name is Ana.
Picture 4: Glad to meet you.
Picture 5: What country are you from?

THE ENGLISH ALPHABET

There are 26 letters in English. Learn to spell your name in English.

	Printed in Books		Printed by Hand		Written	
	Capital	Small	Capital	Small	Capital	Small
1.	A	a	A	a	*a*	*a*
2.	B	b	B	b	*B*	*b*
3.	C	c	C	c	*C*	*c*
4.	D	d	D	d	*D*	*d*
5.	E	e	E	e	*E*	*e*
6.	F	f	F	f	*F*	*f*
7.	G	g	G	g	*G*	*g*
8.	H	h	H	h	*H*	*h*
9.	I	i	I	i	*I*	*i*
10.	J	j	J	j	*J*	*j*
11.	K	k	K	k	*K*	*k*
12.	L	l	L	l	*L*	*l*
13.	M	m	M	m	*M*	*m*
14.	N	n	N	n	*N*	*n*
15.	O	o	O	o	*O*	*o*
16.	P	p	P	p	*P*	*p*
17.	Q	q	Q	q	*Q*	*q*
18.	R	r	R	r	*R*	*r*
19.	S	s	S	s	*S*	*s*
20.	T	t	T	t	*T*	*t*
21.	U	u	U	u	*U*	*u*
22.	V	v	V	v	*V*	*v*
23.	W	w	W	w	*W*	*w*
24.	X	x	X	x	*X*	*x*
25.	Y	y	Y	y	*Y*	*y*
26.	Z	z	Z	z	*Z*	*z*

SPEAKING ACTIVITY

Ask some people in your class what their names are. You can say:
> What's your name?
> Please spell it. (or Please write it.)

Write each name in your notebook.

READING AND WRITING: Names and Titles on a Form

Here is Tony's name.

A

Tony	José	Faria
First name	Middle name	Last name

Here is Ana's name.

B

Ana	Sara	Pinto
First name or Given name	Middle name or Given name	Last name or Family name or Surname

C

Here are more names from different countries.

	First name	Middle name	Family name
1.	Nam	Thi	Nguyen
2.	Peter		Kowalski
3.	Samuel	Americo	Rodriguez
4.	Yung Chiang		Su
5.	Inder Pal		Sagoo

D

Fill this form out. Use your own name.

First name	Middle name	Last or Family name.

E

Here is Tony's name again, in block letters.

PRINT IN BLOCK LETTERS										
FAMILY OR LAST NAME	F	A	R	I	A					
FIRST AND MIDDLE NAME	T	O	N	Y		J	O	S	É	

F

Fill this form out. Use your own name.

PRINT IN BLOCK LETTERS												
FAMILY OR LAST NAME												
FIRST AND MIDDLE NAME												

This is Ana's family.

This is Ana Pinto. This is Miss Pinto or Ms. Pinto.

This is Ana's mother, Gladys Pinto. This is Mrs. Pinto or Ms. Pinto.

This is Ana's father, Ricardo Pinto. This is Mr. Pinto.

Learn these titles.

Mr. is pronounced Mister.
Mrs. is pronounced Missuz.
Miss is pronounced Miss.
Ms. is pronounced Miz.

Here is Ana's name and title on a form.

Surname (family name) Please print		Initials	
P I N T O		A S	☐ Miss ☐ Mr. ☐ Mrs. ☑ Ms.

Fill this form out for yourself.

Surname (family name) Please print		Initials	
			☐ Miss ☐ Mr. ☐ Mrs. ☐ Ms.

GRAMMAR: The Verb   Be

I'm Tony

Long form
(for formal writing)

Short form
(for speaking and
informal writing)

The short form: what happens

"**I**" is a personal pronoun.

"**Am**" is a form of the verb **be**.

Pronoun and verb together:

I'm Tony.
I'm from Portugal.

You

Tell about yourself.

I'm Ana.
I'm from Chile.

_____

_____

_____

EXTRA STUDY: Immigration to Ontario

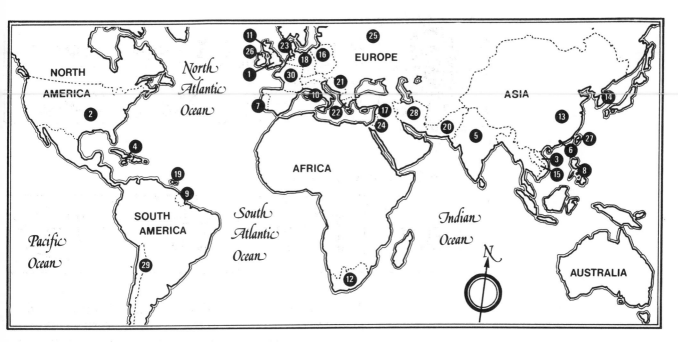

People come to Ontario from many countries. The numbers on the map are the 30 places that most immigrants came from in the years 1977 to 1981. Below are the names of the places. Match the number to the name and put the number in the box. The lower the number, the higher the immigration. For example, 32,788 immigrants came from country number 1 (England), and 1,539 immigrants came from number 30 (France).

29	Chile		Israel		Poland
	China		Italy		Portugal
	England		Jamaica		Scotland
	France		Korea		South Africa
	Germany		Laos		Soviet Union
	Greece		Lebanon		Taiwan
	Guyana		Netherlands		Trinidad-Tobago
	Hong Kong		Northern Ireland		United States
	India		Pakistan		Vietnam
	Iran		Philippines		Yugoslavia

The answers are on page 126.

Spelling Practice

Look at the map on page 7. Write each number in your notebook.

Beside each number, write the name of the country.

Look at the names on page 7. Correct your spelling.

Examples:

1. England
2. U.S.A.

EXTRA STUDY: Crossword Puzzle
Look on page 7, if necessary.

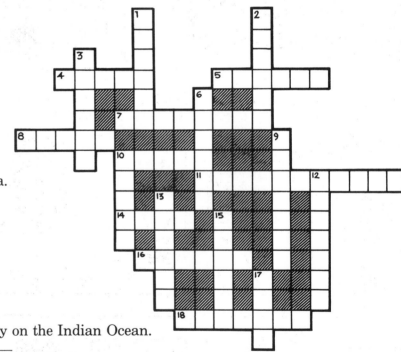

Down
1. Trinidad- ___
2. A country in the Middle East.
3. ___ States.
6. A country in South America.
9. Northern ___
10. Another country in South America.
12. A country on the Mediterranean Sea.
13. A country East of Germany.
15. A country in Europe famous for cuisine.
17. ___ Kong.

Across
4. A country on the Indian Ocean.
5. United ___
7. A country on the Atlantic Ocean, west of Spain.
8. A country near Japan.
10. A large country in Asia.
11. A country in Europe on the North Sea.
14. A country in Asia between Thailand and Vietnam.
16. A country near Hong Kong.
18. A country on the South China Sea.

The answers are on **page 126.**

UNIT 2: GETTING CHANGE

VOCABULARY: For the Conversation

coffee

change

CONVERSATION: Ana Asks for Change

First, look at ALL the pictures. Then look at EACH picture.
WHAT IS THE PERSON SAYING? TRY TO GUESS.

WORDS FOR THE CONVERSATION

Do you have change?

Yes. Here.

Thank you.

You're welcome.

Other Sentences You May Hear

Picture 1: Can you give me change?
　　　　　Can you give me change for a dollar?
　　　　　Can you change a dollar?
Picture 2: Yes. Here you are.
Picture 3: Thanks. (INFORMAL)

READING: Coffee Machine

Which buttons do you press on the coffee machine?
Match the word(s) to the picture and put the letter in the box.

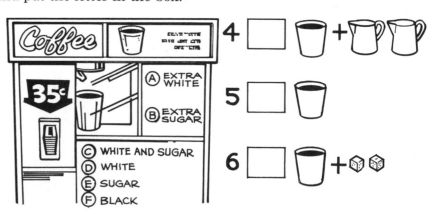

The answers are on page 126.

VOCABULARY: Coins and Bills

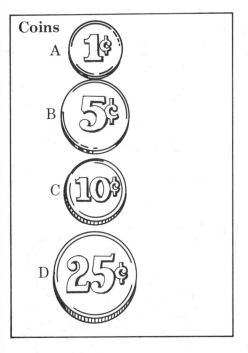

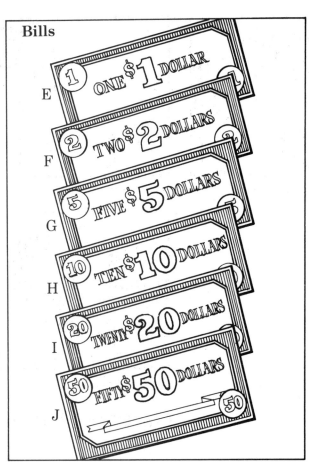

A. a cent or a penny
B. a nickel
C. a dime
D. a quarter
E. a dollar bill
F. a two-dollar bill
G. a five-dollar bill
H. a ten-dollar bill
I. a twenty-dollar bill
J. a fifty-dollar bill

COMMUNICATION ACTIVITY: Getting Change

Ask other people in the class for change. You can say:
Do you have change for (a dollar)?

The other person answers:
Yes. Here.   or   **No. I'm sorry. I don't.**

NUMBERS: Zero to One Hundred

A. Numbers Zero to Thirty-Nine

0 Zero	10 Ten	20 Twenty	30 Thirty
1 One	11 Eleven	21 Twenty-one	31 Thirty-one
2 Two	12 Twelve	22 Twenty-two	32 Thirty-two
3 Three	13 Thirteen	23 Twenty-three	33 Thirty-three
4 Four	14 Fourteen	24 Twenty-four	34 Thirty-four
5 Five	15 Fifteen	25 Twenty-five	35 Thirty-five
6 Six	16 Sixteen	26 Twenty-six	36 Thirty-six
7 Seven	17 Seventeen	27 Twenty-seven	37 Thirty-seven
8 Eight	18 Eighteen	28 Twenty-eight	38 Thirty-eight
9 Nine	19 Nineteen	29 Twenty-nine	39 Thirty-nine

B. Numbers Forty to One Hundred

40 Forty	50 Fifty	60 Sixty	70 Seventy
80 Eighty	90 Ninety	100 One Hundred	

PRONUNCIATION

13 and 30 sound almost the same. Listen. Which do you hear, a or b? Write a or b.

$13.00

$30.00

1. _____ 2. _____ 3. _____ 4. _____ 5. _____ 6. _____ 7. _____ 8. _____

If you don't know whether someone is saying 13 or 30, ask:
Is that **one three** or **three zero**?

GRAMMAR: Questions with Do

1. Ana is asking
   a question.

Do you have change?

2. This is how you make
   a question.
   a. Take the words

you | have | change

b. Add the word **do**.

Do | you | have | change | ?

3. Make questions.

a

Do you have a quarter ?

b

c

d

The answers are on **page 126**.

EXTRA STUDY: Writing Cheques

A

Ana bought a book at Black's Bookstore for $11.95. Here is the cheque she wrote.

THE BANK OF BELLEVILLE
109 WATER STREET

PAY TO THE ORDER OF

Feb. 11 19 84

Black's Bookstore $ 11.$\frac{95}{00}$

Eliven ——————————— $\frac{95}{00}$ DOLLARS

RE 16501   *Ana Pinto*

B You bought a book at Black's Bookstore for $8.00 Complete this cheque.

THE BANK OF BELLEVILLE
109 WATER STREET

PAY TO THE ORDER OF

Feb. 25 19 84

_____ $ _____

_____ DOLLARS

RE 15942   _____

Write these amounts

C $18.95

Black's Bookstore $ _____

_____ DOLLARS

D $22.00

Black's Bookstore $ _____

_____ DOLLARS

E $42.50

Black's Bookstore $ _____

_____ DOLLARS

Check your spelling of the amounts on page 12.

UNIT 3: PERSONAL IDENTIFICATION

VOCABULARY: For the Conversation

(to) work

(to) work

Ana lives at
21 King St.
Betty lives at 23.

number

King Street

CONVERSATION: Walking Home

First, look at ALL the pictures. Then look at EACH picture.
WHAT IS THE PERSON SAYING? TRY TO GUESS.

15

Where do you live?

On King Street.

Really? I work on King Street.

What number?

Forty.

I live at number twenty-one.

Other Sentences You May Hear

Picture 1: What street do you live on?
Picture 3: I have a job on King Street.
I'm working on King Street.

PRONUNCIATION

I. **Walk** and **work** sound almost the same.
Listen. Which do you hear, a or b ?

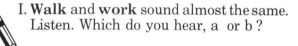

a

I walk
on King St.

b

I work
on King St.

1. _____ 2. _____ 3. _____ 4. _____ 5. _____ 6. _____ 7. _____ 8. _____

II. **14** and **40** sound almost the same.
Listen. Which do you hear, a or b ?

a

14 King Street

b

40 King Street

1. _____ 2. _____ 3. _____ 4. _____ 5. _____ 6. _____ 7. _____ 8. _____

If people don't hear you, say each digit separately:
14 **one four**   40 **four zero**

16

READING AND WRITING: Addresses

Ana lives in a house at 21 King Street.

Tony lives in an apartment building at 400 Simcoe Street.

Tony's apartment number is 3.

Where do you live, in a house or an apartment? _____

Tony received a letter from his friend Samuel. This is the envelope.

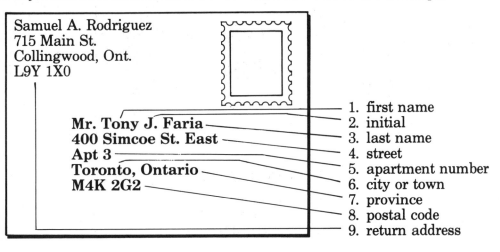

Samuel A. Rodriguez
715 Main St.
Collingwood, Ont.
L9Y 1X0

Mr. Tony J. Faria
400 Simcoe St. East
Apt 3
Toronto, Ontario
M4K 2G2

1. first name
2. initial
3. last name
4. street
5. apartment number
6. city or town
7. province
8. postal code
9. return address

You have written a letter to Tony. Write the envelope for it.
Use your own return address.

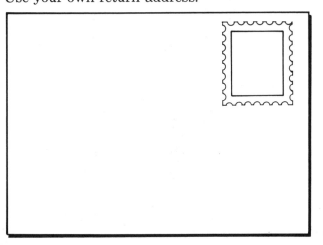

Tony filled out these forms.

A

PLEASE PRINT ☑ Mr. ☐ Mrs. ☐ Miss ☐ Ms.

Tony	J.	Faria
First Name	Initial	Last Name
400	Simcoe St. E.	3
Number	Street	Apt. Number
Toronto		Ontario
City or Town		Province
		M4K 2G2
		Postal Code

B

PLEASE PRINT ☑ Mr. ☐ Mrs. ☐ Miss ☐ Ms.

NAME	Tony J. Faria
ADDRESS	400 Simcoe St. E, Apt. 3
CITY AND PROVINCE	Toronto, Ontario
POSTAL CODE	M4K 2G2

Fill out these forms with information about yourself.

C

PLEASE PRINT ☐ Mr. ☐ Mrs. ☐ Miss ☐ Ms.

First Name	Initial	Last Name
Number	Street	Apt. Number
City or Town		Province
		Postal Code

D

PLEASE PRINT ☐ Mr. ☐ Mrs. ☐ Miss ☐ Ms.

NAME	
ADDRESS	
CITY AND PROVINCE	
POSTAL CODE	

SPEAKING ACTIVITY

Ask some people their name and where they live. You can say:
What's your name? Where do you live, in a house or apartment?

Write each name here and check (✓) **house** or **apartment**.

Name	House	Apartment	Name	House	Apartment
Ana	✓				
Tony		✓			

GRAMMAR: Questions with Where

1. Tony is asking a question.

Where do you live?

2. There are two kinds of questions.

Yes or no questions:	Do	you	have change?	Answers:	Yes or No
	Do	you	work on King St.?		
Question-word questions:	Where do	you	live?	Answers:	on Simcoe St.
	Where do	you	work?		on King St.

3. **Make question-word questions.**   **Make statements.**

a

Where do you live ?

b

I live on King Street.

c

Where do you work ?

d

— — — — — —

e

— — — — — —

f

— — — — — —

g

— — — — — —

h

— — — — — —

The answers are on page 126.

...n the dictionary, if necessary.

Down
1. The name of this country.
3. The language you are learning.
5. The number after ten.
6. The number after eleven.

Across
2. The number and name of your street is your ___.
4. The opposite of "yes."
5. The number before nine.
7. The number before ten.
8. "She" is a feminine pronoun. ___ is a masculine pronoun.

The answers are on **page 126**.

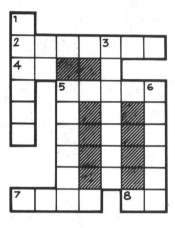

EXTRA STUDY: Kinds of Streets and Abbreviations

Tony lives on Simcoe Street. "St." is the abbreviation for "Street." We use the abbreviation when we write an address.

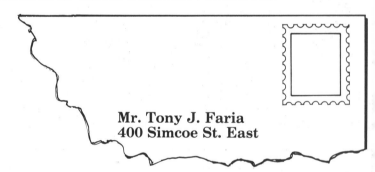

Mr. Tony J. Faria
400 Simcoe St. East

Here are kinds of streets.

A. Street
or
B. Road

C. Avenue
or
D. Boulevard

E. Crescent

F. Court
or
G. Square

Here are the abbreviations. Match the kind of street to the abbreviation.

1 [D] Blvd.   4 [ ] St.   7 [ ] Rd.
2 [ ] Sq.   5 [ ] Ave.   8 [ ] Cres.
3 [ ] Crt.   6 [ ] R.R.

H. Rural Route

UNIT 4: INTRODUCTION OF OTHERS

CONVERSATION: Ana Meets Lou

Ana

Lou

First, look at ALL the pictures. Then look at EACH picture.
WHAT IS THE PERSON SAYING? TRY TO GUESS.

WORDS FOR THE CONVERSATION

1 Hello Ana.

2 How are you?

3 Fine thanks.

4 How are you?

5 Fine.

6 This is Lou.

7 Lou, this is Ana.

8 Nice to meet you.

9 Oh.

10 I'm sorry.

11 That's okay.

Other Sentences You May Hear

Picture 7: Lou, I'd like you to meet Ana.
Picture 8: Glad to meet you.
　　　　　Pleased to meet you.
　　　　　Hi. (INFORMAL)
　　　　　Hello.
Picture 11: That's all right.

EXTENSION WITH CHOICES: Introducing Others

Make two
conversations.

1. This is Lou.

2. Lou, this is Ana.

3. She's from Chile.
4. She's in my class.

5. Nice to meet you.

Here is one conversation from the Extension.

Tony: 1. This is Lou.
2. Lou this is Ana.
3. She's from Chile.
Ana: 5. Nice to meet you.

Look at the Extension and write another conversation in your notebook.
The second conversation is on page 126.

COMMUNICATION ACTIVITY: Photos From Home

Bring a photograph of someone to class. Tell who that person is and say one thing about
him or her, for example:

This is my friend.   This is Albert Einstein.
She's from Laos.   He's a famous scientist.

USEFUL INFORMATION: Social Insurance Number

1

Tony has a social insurance card.

2

His social insurance number (SIN) is on the card.

3

He needs the number to work.

4

He needs the number for unemployment insurance.

5

Lou has a social insurance number, too.

READING AND WRITING:
Application for a Social Insurance Number

Lou got his application for a social insurance card at a Canada Employment Centre. Here is part of the form.

1 FIRST NAME Hsi An (Lou)	MIDDLE NAME	PRESENT FAMILY NAME (SURNAME) Wong

2 DATE OF BIRTH	DAY MONTH YEAR 3 8 44	DO NOT WRITE HERE	3		4 SEX	MALE ✓	FEMALE

5 PLACE OF BIRTH Canton, China	6 SURNAME AT BIRTH Wong	7

8 FATHER'S FIRST NAME Wu Liu	9 HAVE YOU EVER BEFORE APPLIED FOR OR RECEIVED A SOCIAL INSURANCE NUMBER	YES	NO ✓	10 IF "YES" WRITE YOUR NUMBER HERE		DON'T KNOW

11 DATE 2/4/75	12 MARITAL STATUS	SINGLE	MARRIED ✓	OTHER	13 STATUS IN CANADA	CANADIAN CITIZEN ✓	PERMANENT RESIDENT	OTHER

14 APPLICANT'S WRITTEN SIGNATURE Lou Wong

Fill this out with information about yourself.

1 FIRST NAME	MIDDLE NAME	PRESENT FAMILY NAME (SURNAME)

2 DATE OF BIRTH	DAY MONTH YEAR	DO NOT WRITE HERE	3		4 SEX	MALE	FEMALE

5 PLACE OF BIRTH	6 SURNAME AT BIRTH	7

8 FATHER'S FIRST NAME	9 HAVE YOU EVER BEFORE APPLIED FOR OR RECEIVED A SOCIAL INSURANCE NUMBER	YES	NO	10 IF "YES" WRITE YOUR NUMBER HERE		DON'T KNOW

11 DATE	12 MARITAL STATUS	SINGLE	MARRIED	OTHER	13 STATUS IN CANADA	CANADIAN CITIZEN	PERMANENT RESIDENT	OTHER

14 APPLICANT'S WRITTEN SIGNATURE

GRAMMAR: The Verb   Be

She's from Chile.

Long form
(for formal writing)

| She | is | from Chile. |

Short form
(for speaking and
informal writing)

| She's | from Chile. |

2 The short form: what happens

3 **She** and **he**
are personal pronouns.

Is is a form of
the verb **be**.

Pronoun
and verb together:

| She is | She's |
| He is | He's |

4 Make sentences.

She's from Chile.

b.

_____ _____ _____

e.

_____ _____ _____

c.

_____ _____ _____ _____

f.

_____ _____ _____ _____

The answers are on page 126.

25

PRONUNCIATION

1. Look at this word. It has two parts. The parts are called syllables.

2. The first part or syllable is strong. We say it louder.

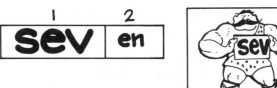

3. Look at this word. It has three syllables. The second syllable is strong. We say it louder.

4. The first syllable of these words is strong:

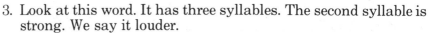

5. The second syllable of these words is strong:

 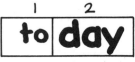

6. Listen to these words. Circle the number of the strong syllable.

a. ① 2 **seven**

b. 1 ② 3 **apartment**

c. 1 2 **coffee**

d. 1 2 3 **example**

e. 1 2 **seven**

f. 1 2 **dollar**

g. 1 2 **sorry**

h. 1 2 3 **important**

i. 1 2 **quarter**

j. 1 2 3 **initial**

k. 1 2 3 **insurance**

The answers are on page 126.

26

EXTRA STUDY: The Family

This is Lou's family.

1. I'm Lou.

A is my brother.
B is my mother.
C is my father.
D is my wife.
F is my son.
G is my son.

2. I'm Lou's brother.

G is my nephew.
F is my nephew.
D is my sister-in-law.

Complete these sentences.

3. I'm Lou's son.

A is my ___uncle___

B is my _____

C is my _____

D is my _____

E is my _____

G is my _____

grandfather
mother
father
grandmother
uncle
brother

4. I'm Lou's mother.

A is my _____

C is my _____

D is my _____

F is my _____

G is my _____

daughter-in-law
husband
son
grandson
grandson

The answers are on page 127.

27

EXTRA STUDY: Crossword Puzzle

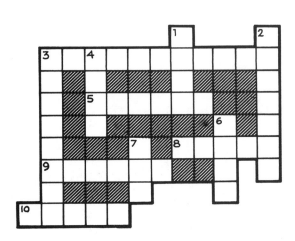

Down
1. My __ is Ana.
2. This person (male) has the same mother and father as you.
3. Son of your son or daughter.
4. Sister of your mother or father.
6. Nice to __ you.
7. The number after nine.

Across
3. Father of your father or mother.
5. Son of your brother or sister.
8. Daughter of your brother or sister.
9. This person (female) has the same mother and father as you.
10. Brother of your mother or father.

The answers are on **page 127**.

EXTRA STUDY: Two-line Dialogues

Complete each dialogue.

1. [D] I'm Ana.

   <u>Nice to meet you.</u>

2. [   ] Where are you from?

   _____

3. [   ] Do you have change for a dollar?

   _____

4. [   ] Where do you live?

   _____

5. [   ] How are you?

   _____

6. [   ] Your address please?

   _____

7. [   ] Your telephone number?

   _____

Choose from these sentences.

A. Yes. Here.
B. Chile.
C. Fine thanks.
D. Nice to meet you.
E. On King St.
F. 751-2632.
G. 42 Main St. West.

The answers are on page 127.

VOCABULARY: For the Conversation

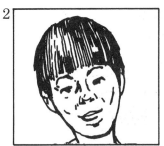

1. ambulance
2. boy
3. hurt
4. address
5. house

6. apartment
7. number
8. apartment number
9. telephone number
10. name

CONVERSATION: Lou Calls Emergency

a
Lou

b
Ken

c
Su Ping

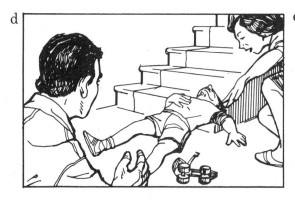

CONVERSATION

First, look at ALL the pictures. Then look at EACH picture.
WHAT IS THE PERSON SAYING? TRY TO GUESS.

WORDS FOR THE CONVERSATION

1 Emergency.

2 Ambulance, please.

3 My boy is hurt.

4 Your address please?

5 42 Main Street West.

6 House or apartment?

7 Apartment, number 301.

8 Your telephone number?

9 751-2632.

10 And your name?

11 Lou Wong.

12 Fine.

Other Questions Policeman May Ask
What language do you speak? What's the nearest major intersection? What municipality is that?

32

SPELLING

Can you spell your name and your street name in English?
This is important.

Please spell your address.

M-A-I-N.

Some alphabet letters are difficult to hear. We use familiar
words to help people hear the correct letter.

Please spell it again.

M for Monday -A-I-N.

SPEAKING ACTIVITY

Ask some people in your class to spell their name and the
name of their street. You can say:

Please spell your name.   Please spell the name of your street.

Write each name and the name of the street here. Then show
it to the person. Is it correct?

Ana   King Street

Continue in your notebook.

EMERGENCY TELEPHONE NUMBERS

Write the emergency numbers for your local area. They are
in the front of your telephone book.

Fire Department

Ambulance

Police

Poison Information
Centre

USEFUL INFORMATION: If Your Child Swallows Poison

1

Your child swallows poison.

2

If someone in your house speaks English,

3

ask that person to call the Poison Information Centre.

4

That person will get important information.

5

If no one in your house speaks English,

6

call an ambulance.

7

Take your child AND the poison container.

8

The ambulance will take you to the Emergency Department of the nearest hospital.

9

Show the poison container.

For more useful information, read "Newcomers Guide to Services in Ontario." This booklet is free and comes in different languages. It is published by the Ministry of Citizenship and Culture. For information or help, go to an immigrant aid agency. Look in your telephone directory under the name of your nationality, for example "Italian" or "Vietnamese."

USEFUL INFORMATION: The Fire Department

You call the fire department

if you have a fire

or a gas leak

or if someone is stuck.

PRONUNCIATION

Here are the names of streets you can find in some Ontario cities. Listen to each name and circle the number of the strong syllable.

a. ① 2 | Hur on | St.

b. 1 ② 3 4 | On tar i o | Ave.

c. 1 2 3 | Mc Ken zie | St.

d. 1 2 | Sim coe | St.

e. 1 2 3 4 | Ni a ga ra | Ave.

f. 1 2 3 | Av e nue | Rd.

g. 1 2 3 4 | Vic tor i a | Ave.

h. 1 2 3 4 | E liz a beth | St.

i. 1 2 | Riv er | St.

j. 1 2 3 | Mac Don ald | St.

k. 1 2 | Col lege | St.

The answers are on page 127.

Write the name of the street you live on. _____

Write the name of the street your school is on. _____

Write the name of two or three streets you use when you come to

school. _____ _____ _____

In each street name, show the strongest syllable. Ask your teacher to help you.

UNIT 6: SAYING HOW YOU FEEL

VOCABULARY: For the Conversation

1. tired
2. hospital
3. big
4. little
5. stairs
6. fall down
7. fine

CONVERSATION: Lou is Tired

a

b

c

36

First, look at ALL the pictures.
Then look at EACH picture.
WHAT IS THE PERSON SAYING? TRY TO GUESS.

2

3

5

6

WORDS FOR THE CONVERSATION

I'm tired.

Oh! Why?

I was at the hospital until four.

My little boy fell down the stairs.

How is he now?

He's fine.

That's good.

Other Sentences You May Hear

Picture 2: Oh! How come? (INFORMAL)
Picture 5: How's he doing now?
Picture 7: I'm glad.

EXTENSION WITH CHOICES

Make two conversations.

1. How's your little boy?

2. He's fine.

3. He's still in the hospital.

4. That's good.

5. That's too bad.

Here is one conversation from the Extension.

Tony : 1. How's your little boy?

Lou : 2. He's fine.

Tony : 4. That's good.

Look at the Extension and write the other conversation in your notebook.

The second conversation is on page 127.

READING AND WRITING: Ontario Health Insurance Plan

a

Lou has an OHIP card. It has a number on it.

b

At the hospital Lou gave this number.

c

OHIP helps pay the hospital and doctor bills.

d

OHIP doesn't pay for dental care, except in hospitals.

Lou filled out an application for OHIP. Here are parts of the form.

❶ Surname (family name) Please print	Initials
W O N G	H A

☐ Miss ☑ Mr. ☐ Mrs. ☐ Ms.

Street address	Insert the name by which you are known e.g. Tom, Vera, etc.
4 2 M A I N S T W	L O U

Apt. no.	Name of City/Town, etc.	Telephone Number — 751-2632
3 0 1	T O R O N T O	

Province	Postal code	Date of Birth	Day 3	Month 8	Year 4 4
O N T A R I O	M 3 Q 4 M 4				

Name of present employer	Previous OHIP no. (if any)	Marital status
SELF – EMPLOYED		☑ Married ☐ Divorced ☐ Widowed ☐ Single ☐ Separated ☐ Other

Insurable status
❷ ☐ **Single premium** I have no eligible dependent(s). ☑ **Family premium** I have eligible dependent(s)

(Dependents are not covered if not residing in Ontario, except as indicated in part **2** on the reverse side of the application)

Fill this out with information about yourself.

❶ Surname (family name) Please print	Initials

☐ Miss ☐ Mr. ☐ Mrs. ☐ Ms.

Street address	Insert the name by which you are known e.g. Tom, Vera, etc.

Apt. no.	Name of City/Town, etc.	Telephone Number —

Province	Postal code	Date of Birth	Day	Month	Year

Name of present employer	Previous OHIP no. (if any)	Marital status
		☐ Married ☐ Divorced ☐ Widowed ☐ Single ☐ Separated ☐ Other

Insurable status
❷ ☐ **Single premium** I have no eligible dependent(s). ☐ **Family premium** I have eligible dependent(s)

(Dependents are not covered if not residing in Ontario, except as indicated in part **2** on the reverse side of the application)

Have you applied for OHIP yet? There is usually a three-month waiting period after you apply. You may receive help to pay your premiums if you do not have enough money.

GRAMMAR: Past Form of the Verb   Be

I'm at work now.

I was at the hospital until four last night.

2 **Was** is a past form of the verb **Be**. It is used with the pronouns: **I, He, She.**

He was at the hospital last night.

She was at the hospital last night.

Lou was at the hospital last night.

3 Make sentences with **Was.**

a.

He was at the hospital last night.

d.

_____

b.

_____

e.

_____

c.

_____

f.

_____

Tell about yourself.

I .... last night.

The answers are on page 127.

USEFUL INFORMATION: Finding a Doctor or Dentist

1. Do you need a doctor or dentist?

2. It's best to ask your friends for the name of a good one.

3. If your friends can't help you, here are other things you can do.

4. The College of Family Physicians has names of family doctors.

5. They will tell you what languages each doctor speaks.

ITALIANO
ESPAÑOL
VIET-NAM
ΕΛΛΗΝΙΚΑ

6. You can also see a doctor in an out-patients clinic at a hospital.

7. The Ontario Dental Association has names of dentists near your home.

8. If a doctor or dentist suggests treatment

9. that you are not sure about, ask questions.

10. You can also go to another doctor or dentist

11. and get another opinion.

12. In a medical or dental emergency, go to a hospital.

42

EXTRA STUDY: Crossword Puzzle

Look in the dictionary if necessary.

Down
2. A place for sick people.
3. A male child.
4. "He" is a masculine pronoun.
   — is a feminine pronoun.
5. The number after eleven.
6. A word to show surprise.
10. A word meaning "okay."
11. The opposite of "little."

Across
1. The opposite of "this."
5. That's — bad.
7. The opposite of "that."
8. A question word meaning "What's the reason?"
9. The opposite of "big."
11. The opposite of "good."
12. "Till" is the short form of —.

The answers are on page 127.

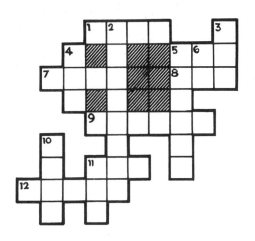

PRONUNCIATION

Is and **was** sometimes sound almost the same. Listen. Which do you hear, a or b? Write a or b.

now
a   He's at the hospital.

last night
b   He was at the hospital.

1. _____   2. _____   3. _____   4. _____   5. _____   6. _____   7. _____   8. _____

BINGO GAME

a. Choose 24 items from the list below. Write one item, in pencil, into each box on the Bingo card. Do this in random order.

b. Listen. When you hear an item, put a check mark in pencil beside it or cover it with a marker.

c. When you have a row of items checked — either vertical, horizontal or diagonal, call out "Bingo" in a loud voice.

$14.00	She's at school.	1403 Main St.
$40.00	She was at school.	1413 Main St.
$ 1.15	How is he?	17 King St.
$ 1.50	How was he?	70 King St.
Queen St.	East	$16.60
Main St.	West	$60.16
walk	He's from Chile.	She's fine.
work	She's from Chile.	She's five.
first name	He's Tony.	
last name	He is Tony.	

		■		

UNIT 7: TELLING THE TIME

CONVERSATION: Lou Asks for the Time

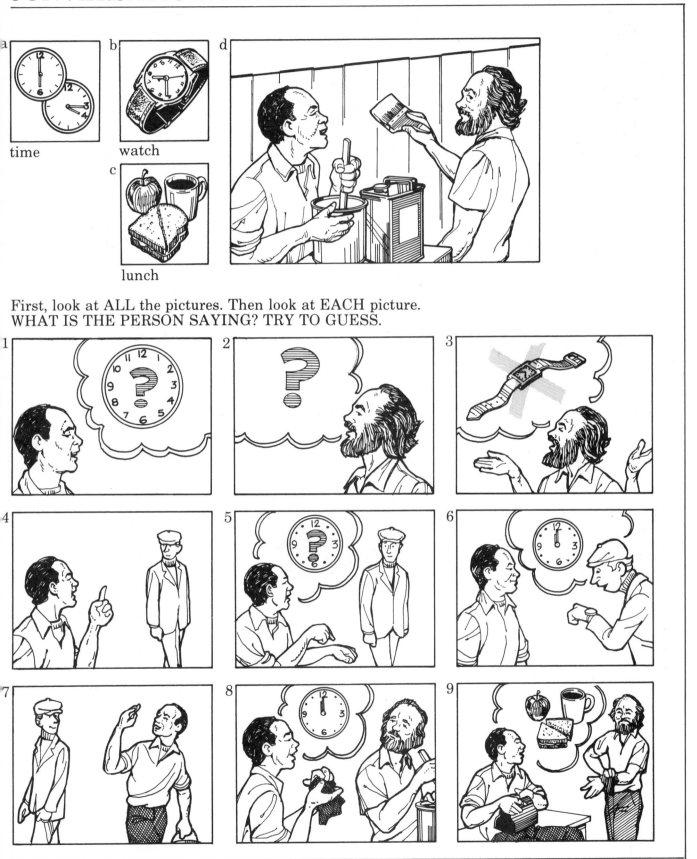

a time

b watch

c lunch

First, look at ALL the pictures. Then look at EACH picture.
WHAT IS THE PERSON SAYING? TRY TO GUESS.

WORDS FOR THE CONVERSATION

What time is it?

I don't know.

I don't have my watch.

Excuse me.

Do you have the time?

It's twelve o'clock.

Thank you.

It's twelve o'clock.

Time for lunch.

Other Sentences You May Hear

Picture 1: What's the time?
What time do you have?
Picture 5: Could you tell me the time, please? (MORE FORMAL)

CLOCK TIMES AROUND THE WORLD

Look at the clocks below. The time on each clock is ahead of the time on the Ottawa clock. For example, the time in Rome, Italy is 6 hours ahead of the time in Ottawa. The time in Seoul, Korea is 14 hours ahead of the time in Ottawa.

What time is it? Complete each sentence.

1.

It's one o'clock in Ottawa, Canada.

It's . . . in Rome, Italy.

It's . . . in London, England.

It's . . . in Lisbon, Portugal.

2.

It's eight-thirty in Ottawa, Canada.

It's . . . in Athens, Greece.

It's . . . in Seoul, Korea.

It's . . . in Warsaw, Poland.

3.

It's ten to nine in Ottawa, Canada.

It's . . . in Belgrade, Yugoslavia.

It's . . . in Jerusalem, Israel.

It's . . . in Islamabad, Pakistan.

4.

It's twenty after four in Ottawa, Canada.

It's . . . in Beirut, Lebanon.

It's . . . in Rome, Italy.

It's . . . in London, England.

5.

It's a quarter to five in Ottawa, Canada.

It's . . . in Lisbon, Portugal.

It's . . . in Athens, Greece.

It's . . . in Seoul, Korea.

47

TELLING TIME

Practise telling the time.

 A   eight o'clock

 B   two minutes   after}   eight
                       past }

 C   five   after}   eight
            past }

 D   ten   after}   eight
           past }

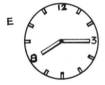 E   a quarter   after}   eight
                past }

 F   twenty   after}   eight
             past }

 G   twenty-five   after}   eight
                   past }

 H   eight-thirty
       or
       half past eight

 I   twenty-five to nine

 J   twenty to nine

 K   a quarter to nine

 L   fourteen minutes to nine

 M   ten to nine

 N   five to nine

 O   three minutes to nine

 P   nine o'clock

What time is it? Listen. Draw the hands to show the time.

A, B, C, D, E, F, G, H, I, J (clock faces)

Digital Clocks
Sometimes people tell the time this way.

5:00 five o'clock	L **5:05** five-o-five	M **5:15** five-fifteen
5:30 five-thirty	O **5:45** five forty-five	P **5:52** five fifty-two

PRONUNCIATION

Listen to the teacher. Circle what you hear, a or b.

1.a. 9:40   4.a. 2:40   7.a. It's 7:30.   10.a. The time is 11:30.
  b. 9:14   b. 2:14   b. It's 7:13.   b. The time is 11:13.

2.a. 9:40   5.a. 2:40   8.a. It's 7:30.   11.a. The time is 11:30.
  b. 9:14   b. 2:14   b. It's 7:13.   b. The time is 11:13.

3.a. 9:40   6.a. 2:40   9.a. It's 7:30.   12.a. The time is 11:30.
  b. 9:14   b. 2:14   b. It's 7:13.   b. The time is 11:13.

THE TIME OF DAY: Morning, Afternoon and Evening

Read this section and answer the questions.

1 It's morning.

2 Lou wakes up at seven a.m. What time do you wake up?

_____

3 Lou works from 8-12. What do you do in the morning?

_____

4 It's 12 noon.

5 Lou eats lunch at noon. What time do you eat lunch?

_____

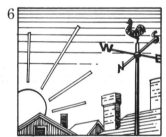

6 It's afternoon.

7 Lou works in the afternoon from one to five.

8 It's evening.

9 Sometimes Lou reads or watches television.

10 Sometimes he visits friends. What do you do in the evening?

_____

11 It's 12:00 midnight.

12 Lou goes to bed around midnight. What time do you go to bed?

_____

50

GRAMMAR: Negative Sentences with Don't

I don't know.
I don't have
my watch.

Long form

Short form

I don't know.

2 The short form: what happens

3 These are **AFFIRMATIVE** sentences.

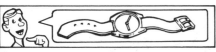

These are **NEGATIVE** sentences.

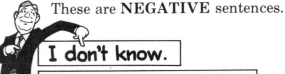

4 Make sentences.

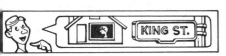

e.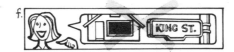

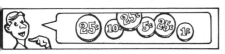

f.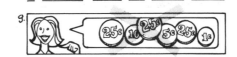

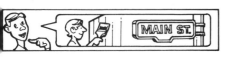

g.

h.

The answers are on page 127.

EXTRA STUDY: Personal Journal

Copy and complete this personal journal to show your typical Saturday.

On Saturday I usually wake up at _____ . In the morning I _____ . Then I eat lunch at _____ . In the afternoon I usually _____ . I eat supper at _____ . In the evening I usually _____ .

EXTRA STUDY: Kinds of Clocks

Match the picture to the word and put the letter in the box.

1 [e] alarm clock   5 [ ] clock radio

2 [ ] digital clock   6 [ ] wall clock

3 [ ] digital watch   7 [ ] cuckoo clock

4 [ ] pocket watch   8 [ ] grandfather clock

The answers are on page 127.

Say each word. The syllable written in dark letters is the strong syllable.

a**larm** **dig**ital **pock**et **ra**dio **cuck**oo **grand**father

Take a partner. You can ask and answer these questions.

Do you have {
an alarm clock?
a digital clock?
a digital watch?
etc.

Where was it made?
or
What country was it made in?

UNIT 8: GETTING HELP WITH ENGLISH

CONVERSATION: Tony Asks Lou for Help

Lou

Tony

First, look at ALL the pictures. Then look at EACH picture.
WHAT IS THE PERSON SAYING? TRY TO GUESS.

2

3

5

6

WORDS FOR THE CONVERSATION

What does this word mean?

Oh. I understand.

Do you have a pencil?

Yes. Here.

Thanks.

Other Sentences You May Hear

Picture 1: I don't understand this word.
Picture 2: Oh. I see.
Picture 3: Do you have a pencil I could borrow? (MORE FORMAL)
　　　　　Could you please lend me a pencil? (MORE FORMAL)

EXTENSION WITH CHOICES: Getting Help with English

Make four conversations.

1. What's your address?

2. 42 Main Street West.

3. Pardon?

4. Please repeat that.

5. Please speak louder.

6. Please speak slowly.

7. 42 Main Street West.

8. **42 MAIN STREET WEST.**

9. 42 Main Street West.

PRONUNCIATION: Review of Alphabet Letters

1. These letters rhyme: A   J   K
2. These letters rhyme: B   C   D   E   G   P   T   V
3. These letters start with the same sound: F   L   M   N   S   X
4. These letters rhyme: I   Y
5. These letters rhyme: Q   U   W
6. These letters don't rhyme: H   O   R   Z

Take a partner. One of you says a letter. The other one points to it.

Listen. Circle the letter or letters you hear.
In numbers 13-30, watch your teacher's mouth.

1. a e	7. i e	13. m n	19. f s	25. v b
2. a e	8. i e	14. m n	20. f s	26. v b
3. a e	9. i e	15. m n	21. f s	27. v b
4. ae ea	10. ie ei	16. mn nm	22. fs sf	28. vb bv
5. ae ea	11. ie ei	17. mn nm	23. fs sf	29. vb bv
6. ae ea	12. ie ei	18. mn nm	24. fs sf	30. vb bv

SPEAKING ACTIVITY: Asking for Help with the Alphabet

Take a partner. One of you is A. The other one is B. Fold this page in half.

A.

Each word below has one letter which is difficult to read. Point to that letter and say:

What's this letter?

Print the word.

1. *work*   ✎ work _____
2. *tired*   _____
3. *twelve*   _____
4. *Chile*   _____
5. *Ontario*   _____
6. *Toronto*   _____
7. *sixteen*   _____
8. *forty*   _____
9. *Quebec*   _____

B.

Look at your partner's difficult letter. Find that letter here. Your partner doesn't look here. Tell your partner the name of the letter.

1. **work**
2. **tired**
3. **twelve**
4. **Chile**
5. **Ontario**
6. **Toronto**
7. **sixteen**
8. **forty**
9. **Quebec**

Unfold this page. Check to see that you printed the correct letters. Then switch with your partner.

COMMUNICATION ACTIVITY: The Parts of the Body

Take a partner. One of you is A. The other one is B. Fold this page in half.

A. You want to know the names of the parts of the body. Look at each picture here; point to that part of your own body and ask your partner for the name. You can say:
What's this called?
and
Please spell it.
Write each name under the picture.

B. When your partner points to a part of the body, look at the picture here and answer your partner with the name.

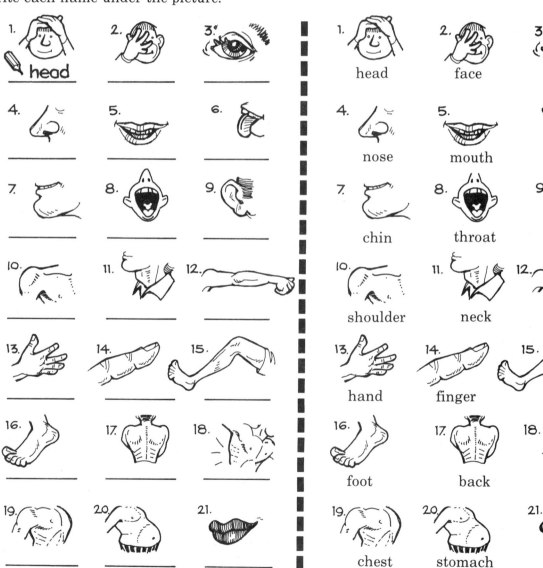

A.

1. head
2.
3.
4.
5.
6.
7.
8.
9.
10.
11.
12.
13.
14.
15.
16.
17.
18.
19.
20.
21.

B.

1. head
2. face
3. eye
4. nose
5. mouth
6. tongue
7. chin
8. throat
9. ear
10. shoulder
11. neck
12. arm
13. hand
14. finger
15. leg
16. foot
17. back
18. side
19. chest
20. stomach
21. lips

Unfold this page. Check your spelling. Then switch with your partner.

Asking for Help with Pronunciation

Some of the words on page 58 are difficult to pronounce, for example:

shoulder, Number 10   mouth, Number 5   chest, Number 19

Ask the teacher to help you with the pronunciation. Give the teacher the picture number of the word that is difficult for you. You can say:

Please pronounce (Number 10). or **How do you say (Number 10)?** or **How do you pronounce (Number 10)?**

PRONUNCIATION

Here are some words from this unit. Listen to each word and circle the number of the strong syllable.

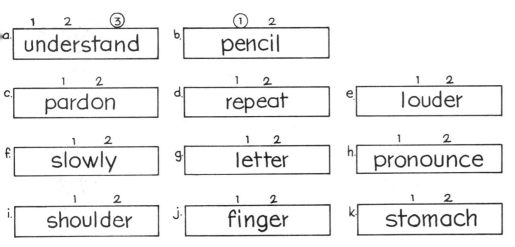

a. ① 2 ③ understand

b. ① 2 pencil

c. 1 2 pardon

d. 1 2 repeat

e. 1 2 louder

f. 1 2 slowly

g. 1 2 letter

h. 1 2 pronounce

i. 1 2 shoulder

j. 1 2 finger

k. 1 2 stomach

The answers are on page 127.

SPEAKING ACTIVITY

Take a partner. One of you is A. The other one is B.

A.

Choose a word from below. Say the word to your partner.

head	throat	leg
face	ear	foot
eye	neck	back
nose	shoulder	side
mouth	arm	chest
tongue	hand	stomach
chin	finger	

B.

Respond to A's word with one of these sentences.

A.

Respond to B's sentence.

1. What does that mean?
2. Pardon?
3. Please speak louder.
4. Please spell that.
5. Please write that.
6. Please repeat that.
7. Please say that again.
8. How do you spell that?
9. I don't understand that word.

EXTRA STUDY: Languages of the World

The country that Ana comes from is Chile.
The language that she speaks is Spanish.

Here are some languages.

Afrikaans	Arabic	Chinese	Dutch
English	French	German	Greek
Hebrew	Hindi	Italian	Korean
Lao	Persian	Polish	Portuguese
Punjabi	Russian	Serbo-Croatian	Vietnamese
Spanish	Tagalog	Urdu	

Here are countries from the map on page 7. Write a language
that people speak in each country. Choose from the list above.

Country or Place	Language	Country or Place	Language
1. England	English	16. Poland	
2. United States		17. Lebanon	
3. Vietnam		18. Germany	
4. Jamaica		19. Trinidad-Tobago	
5. India		20. Pakistan	
6. Hong Kong		21. Yugoslavia	
7. Portugal		22. Greece	
8. Philippines		23. Netherlands	
9. Guyana		24. Israel	
10. Italy		25. Soviet Union	
11. Scotland		26. Northern Ireland	
12. South Africa		27. Taiwan	
13. China		28. Iran	
14. Korea		29. Chile	
15. Laos		30. France	

The answers are on page 128.

UNIT 9: TALKING ABOUT CALENDAR TIME

VOCABULARY: For the Conversation

CONVERSATION: A Doctor's Appointment for Ken

First, look at ALL the pictures. Then look at EACH picture.
WHAT IS THE PERSON SAYING? TRY TO GUESS.

 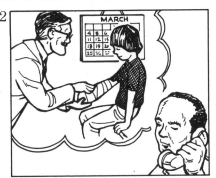 

WORDS FOR THE CONVERSATION

This is Lou Wong.

I'd like an appointment for my little boy.

How about Thursday, March the first at ten a.m.?

I work until four.

How about 4:30 on Monday the fifth?

Okay. That's fine.

Other Sentences You May Hear

Picture 1: This is Lou Wong speaking.
Picture 2: I'd like to have } an appointment for my little boy.
             make }
Picture 3: I can give you Thursday, March first at ten o'clock.

PRONUNCIATION

Tuesday and **Thursday** sound almost the same.

Listen. Which do you hear, a or b? Write a or b.

a
Tuesday

b
Thursday

1. ____ 2. ____ 3. ____ 4. ____ 5. ____ 6. ____ 7. ____ 8. ____ 9. ____

VOCABULARY: The Calendar

A. Ordinal Numbers

First and **fifth** are ordinal numbers. When we say a calendar date we use an ordinal number.

How about Thursday, March the first at ten a.m.?

Match the ordinal number to the cardinal number.

Cardinal Numbers	Ordinal Numbers
one ✏ ___first___	fifth
two ✏ _____	third
three _____	first
four _____	sixth
five _____	second
six _____	fourth
seven _____	tenth
eight _____	ninth
nine _____	eighth
ten _____	seventh

B. Days of the Week

Say the long form. Match it with the short form.

1. Sunday   Tues.
2. Monday   Sat.
3. Tuesday   Sun.
4. Wednesday   Thurs.
5. Thursday   Fri.
6. Friday   Mon.
7. Saturday   Wed.

Jan.						
Sun.	Mon.	Tues.	Wed.	Thurs.	Fri.	Sat.
1	2	3	4	5	6	7
8	9	10	11	12	13	14
15	16	17	18	19	20	21
22	23	24	25	26	27	28
29	30	31				

C. Months of the Year.

On a cheque, you can write the short form or the long form.
Feb. or February

THE BANK OF BELLEVILLE
109 WATER STREET

PAY TO THE
ORDER OF

Feb. 11 19 84

Say the long form.
Look at the calendar.
Copy the short form.

1. January   _Jan._
2. February   _____
3. March   _____
4. April
5. May
6. June
7. July
8. August   _____
9. September   _____
10. October   _____
11. November   _____
12. December   _____

JAN.	FEB.	MAR.
S M T W T F S	S M T W T F S	S M T W T F S
1 2 3 4 5 6 7	1 2 3 4	1 2 3
8 9 10 11 12 13 14	5 6 7 8 9 10 11	4 5 6 7 8 9 10
15 16 17 18 19 20 21	12 13 14 15 16 17 18	11 12 13 14 15 16 17
22 23 24 25 26 27 28	19 20 21 22 23 24 25	18 19 20 21 22 23 24
29 30 31	26 27 28 29	25 26 27 28 29 30 31

APRIL	MAY	JUNE
S M T W T F S	S M T W T F S	S M T W T F S
1 2 3 4 5 6 7	1 2 3 4 5	1 2
8 9 10 11 12 13 14	6 7 8 9 10 11 12	3 4 5 6 7 8 9
15 16 17 18 19 20 21	13 14 15 16 17 18 19	10 11 12 13 14 15 16
22 23 24 25 26 27 28	20 21 22 23 24 25 26	17 18 19 20 21 22 23
29 30	27 28 29 30 31	24 25 26 27 28 29 30

JULY	AUG.	SEPT.
S M T W T F S	S M T W T F S	S M T W T F S
1 2 3 4 5 6 7	1 2 3 4	1
8 9 10 11 12 13 14	5 6 7 8 9 10 11	2 3 4 5 6 7 8
15 16 17 18 19 20 21	12 13 14 15 16 17 18	9 10 11 12 13 14 15
22 23 24 25 26 27 28	19 20 21 22 23 24 25	16 17 18 19 20 21 22
29 30 31	26 27 28 29 30 31	23 30 24 25 26 27 28 29

OCT.	NOV.	DEC.
S M T W T F S	S M T W T F S	S M T W T F S
1 2 3 4 5 6	1 2 3	1
7 8 9 10 11 12 13	4 5 6 7 8 9 10	2 3 4 5 6 7 8
14 15 16 17 18 19 20	11 12 13 14 15 16 17	9 10 11 12 13 14 15
21 22 23 24 25 26 27	18 19 20 21 22 23 24	16 17 18 19 20 21 22
28 29 30 31	25 26 27 28 29 30	23 30 24 31 25 26 27 28 29

LISTENING ACTIVITY: Calendar Dates

Listen. Circle the date you hear.

JAN.	FEB.	MAR.
S M T W T F S	S M T W T F S	S M T W T F S
1 2 3 4 5 6 7	1 2 3 4	1 2 3
8 9 10 11 12 13 14	5 6 7 8 9 10 11	4 5 6 7 8 9 10
15 16 17 18 19 20 21	12 13 14 15 16 17 18	11 12 13 14 15 16 17
22 23 24 25 26 27 28	19 20 21 22 23 24 25	18 19 20 21 22 23 24
29 30 31	26 27 28 29	25 26 27 28 29 30 31

APRIL	MAY	JUNE
S M T W T F S	S M T W T F S	S M T W T F S
1 2 3 4 5 6 7	1 2 3 4 5	1 2
8 9 10 11 12 13 14	6 7 8 9 10 11 12	3 4 5 6 7 8 9
15 16 17 18 19 20 21	13 14 15 16 17 18 19	10 11 12 13 14 15 16
22 23 24 25 26 27 28	20 21 22 23 24 25 26	17 18 19 20 21 22 23
29 30	27 28 29 30 31	24 25 26 27 28 29 30

JULY	AUG.	SEPT.
S M T W T F S	S M T W T F S	S M T W T F S
1 2 3 4 5 6 7	1 2 3 4	1
8 9 10 11 12 13 14	5 6 7 8 9 10 11	2 3 4 5 6 7 8
15 16 17 18 19 20 21	12 13 14 15 16 17 18	9 10 11 12 13 14 15
22 23 24 25 26 27 28	19 20 21 22 23 24 25	16 17 18 19 20 21 22
29 30 31	26 27 28 29 30 31	23 30 24 25 26 27 28 29

OCT.	NOV.	DEC.
S M T W T F S	S M T W T F S	S M T W T F S
1 2 3 4 5 6	1 2 3	1
7 8 9 10 11 12 13	4 5 6 7 8 9 10	2 3 4 5 6 7 8
14 15 16 17 18 19 20	11 12 13 14 15 16 17	9 10 11 12 13 14 15
21 22 23 24 25 26 27	18 19 20 21 22 23 24	16 17 18 19 20 21 22
28 29 30 31	25 26 27 28 29 30	23 30 24 31 25 26 27 28 29

JAN.	FEB.	MAR.
S M T W T F S	S M T W T F S	S M T W T F S
1 2 3 4 5 6 7	1 2 3 4	1 2 3
8 9 10 11 12 13 14	5 6 7 8 9 10 11	4 5 6 7 8 9 10
15 16 17 18 19 20 21	12 13 14 15 16 17 18	11 12 13 14 15 16 17
22 23 24 25 26 27 28	19 20 21 22 23 24 25	18 19 20 21 22 23 24
29 30 31	26 27 28 29	25 26 27 28 29 30 31

APRIL	MAY	JUNE
S M T W T F S	S M T W T F S	S M T W T F S
1 2 3 4 5 6 7	1 2 3 4 5	1 2
8 9 10 11 12 13 14	6 7 8 9 10 11 12	3 4 5 6 7 8 9
15 16 17 18 19 20 21	13 14 15 16 17 18 19	10 11 12 13 14 15 16
22 23 24 25 26 27 28	20 21 22 23 24 25 26	17 18 19 20 21 22 23
29 30	27 28 29 30 31	24 25 26 27 28 29 30

JULY	AUG.	SEPT.
S M T W T F S	S M T W T F S	S M T W T F S
1 2 3 4 5 6 7	1 2 3 4	1
8 9 10 11 12 13 14	5 6 7 8 9 10 11	2 3 4 5 6 7 8
15 16 17 18 19 20 21	12 13 14 15 16 17 18	9 10 11 12 13 14 15
22 23 24 25 26 27 28	19 20 21 22 23 24 25	16 17 18 19 20 21 22
29 30 31	26 27 28 29 30 31	23 30 24 25 26 27 28 29

OCT.	NOV.	DEC.
S M T W T F S	S M T W T F S	S M T W T F S
1 2 3 4 5 6	1 2 3	1
7 8 9 10 11 12 13	4 5 6 7 8 9 10	2 3 4 5 6 7 8
14 15 16 17 18 19 20	11 12 13 14 15 16 17	9 10 11 12 13 14 15
21 22 23 24 25 26 27	18 19 20 21 22 23 24	16 17 18 19 20 21 22
28 29 30 31	25 26 27 28 29 30	23 30 24 31 25 26 27 28 29

SPEAKING ACTIVITY

Ask some people these questions:

A. What's your name? (Please spell it.)
B. When's your birthday?
C. When did you come to Canada?

Write the answers here:

A. NAME	B. BIRTHDAY (Month) (Day)	C. DATE OF ARRIVAL IN CANADA (Month) (Day) (Year)
Tony	June 6	Feb 7 1984

Continue in your notebook.

COMMUNICATION ACTIVITY: Calling for an Appointment

Caller:
Call and ask for an appointment.

Receptionist:
1. Give an appointment time.
2. Ask for the caller's name and telephone number.
3. Write the name and phone number in the appointment book.

THURSDAY, MARCH 1.

TIME	NAME	PHONE NO.
10:00		
10:30		
11:00		
11:30		
12:00		
12:30		
1:00		
1:30		
2:00		
2:30		
3:00		
3:30		
4:00		
4:30		

FRIDAY, MARCH 2.

TIME	NAME	PHONE NO.
10:00		
10:30		
11:00		
11:30		
12:00		
12:30		
1:00		
1:30		
2:00		
2:30		
3:00		
3:30		
4:00		
4:30		

MONDAY, APRIL 2.

TIME	NAME	PHONE NO.
10:00		
10:30		
11:00		
11:30		
12:00		
12:30		
1:00		
1:30		
2:00		
2:30		
3:00		
3:30		
4:00		
4:30		

TUESDAY, APRIL 3.

TIME	NAME	PHONE NO.
10:00		
10:30		
11:00		
11:30		
12:00		
12:30		
1:00		
1:30		
2:00		
2:30		
3:00		
3:30		
4:00		
4:30		

GRAMMAR: Verbs with s Added

This is a statement with **I**.

I work until 4.

I work until four.

This is a statement with **He**.
You add **s** to the verb **work**.

He works until four.

3 This is a statement with **She**.

She works until four.

4 This is a statement with **Tony**.

Tony works on King Street.

5 Make statements.

a.
He works until five.

e.
She lives on King Street.

b.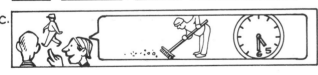
She works until four-thirty.

f.
_____

c.
_____

g.
_____

d.
_____

h.
_____

The answers are on page 128.

67

USEFUL INFORMATION: Holidays and Other Special Days

1

Canada Day is on July 1.

2

On July 1, in 1867, four separate provinces united.

3

Canada became a country.

4

Businesses are closed on July 1.

5

This is a national holiday.

6

In the evening there are fireworks in some of the public parks.

7. These are the national holidays:

New Year's Day, January 1
Good Friday, in March or April
Queen Victoria Day, May 24 or the Monday before
Canada Day, July 1
Labour Day, the first Monday in September
Thanksgiving Day, the second Monday in October
Christmas, December 25

8. This is a provincial holiday in Ontario. Not all businesses are closed:

Lord Simcoe Day, the first Monday in August

9. These are other special days in Canada:

Valentine's Day, February 14
Easter Monday, in March or April
Mother's Day, the second Sunday in May
Father's Day, the third Sunday in June
Hallowe'en, October 31
Remembrance Day, November 11
Boxing Day, December 26

EXTRA STUDY: More About Holidays and Other Special Days

Read silently. Look in the dictionary if necessary.

New Year's Day — January 1
This is a national holiday. The evening of December 31 is called "New Year's Eve." On New Year's Eve there are parties and other celebrations. Exactly at midnight everyone kisses and says "Happy New Year."

Valentine's Day — February 14
The name comes from Saint Valentine. He lived hundreds of years ago. This day is special for people in love. They send greeting cards called "Valentines" or they give gifts. Children often give Valentine cards.

Victoria Day — May 24, or the Monday before
This is the birthday of Queen Victoria; she was the Queen of England for more than 60 years. In the evening there are fireworks in some of the public parks.

Remembrance Day — November 11
We remember the Canadian soldiers who died in World War I and II. Red poppy flowers grew on the graves of soldiers in Belgium. We buy red poppies and the money goes to veteran soldiers.

Labour Day — The first Monday in September
This day honours all workers. There is often a parade on the main street of a city. Labour Day is the last day of summer holidays for children before they return to school.

1 a party

2 a kiss

3 giving a gift

4 a valentine

5 Queen Victoria

6 soldiers

7 a veteran soldier

8 a parade

EXTRA STUDY: Crossword Puzzle

Down

1. After the second.
2. Before the second.
3. The day after Sunday.
4. Sixth month of the year.
5. Short form of "Sunday."
9. Short form of "Saturday."
10. Short form of "August."

Across

2. After the third.
6. After the first.
7. Eighth month of the year.
8. The day after Tuesday.
11. Short form of "February."
12. The day before Saturday.

The answers are on page 128.

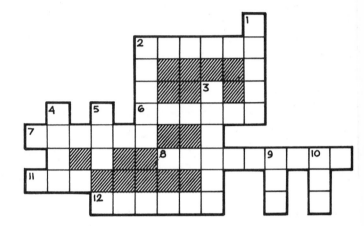

UNIT 10: FINDING YOUR WAY AROUND

CONVERSATION: Lou and Ken Take the Bus

First, look at ALL the pictures. Then look at EACH picture.
WHAT IS THE PERSON SAYING? TRY TO GUESS.

WORDS FOR THE CONVERSATION

1

Do you go to Queen Street?

2

Yes.

3

Please call out Queen Street.

4

Sure.

5

Queen Street next.

6

Thank you.

7

You're welcome.

Other Sentences You May Hear

Picture 1: Does this bus go to Queen Street?
Picture 3: Would you please call out Queen Street?
Picture 4: Okay. I will.
Picture 5: Next stop Queen Street.

READING: Bus Routes

There are three buses on Main Street: 5A, 5B and 5C.

These three buses start out together on Main Street; then they go three different routes.

Here are the three bus routes.

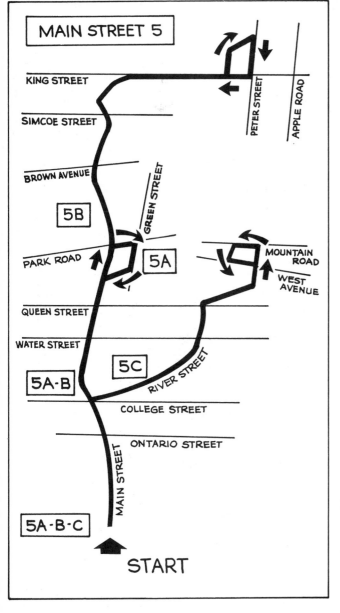

Answer these questions.

1. Does the Number 5A bus go to Queen St.?
   Yes

2. Which bus goes to Brown Ave.?
   5B

3. Does the Number 5C bus go to King St.?
   _____

4. Does the Number 5B go to Simcoe St.?
   _____

5. Which bus goes to West Ave.?
   _____

6. Which bus goes to Green St.?
   _____

7. Does the Number 5B go to Mountain Rd.?
   _____

8. Does the Number 5A go to Park Rd.?
   _____

9. Which bus goes to Peter St.?
   _____

10. Which bus goes to Mountain Rd.?
    _____

11. Does the 5A bus go to King St.?
    _____

The answers are on page 128.

COMMUNICATION ACTIVITY: Asking for the Right Bus

Take a partner. One of you is A. The other one is B.

A

B

You want to get to each street below. Ask your partner for the right bus. You can say:
How do I get to (Queen Street)?
or
What bus do I take to (Queen Street)?

Look at the bus route on page 73. Answer your partner. You can say:
Take the (5A) bus.

 Write down the number of the bus.

Queen Street	_5A-B_	Simcoe Street	_____	West Avenue	_____
Water Street	_____	Park Road	_____	Mountain Road	_____
Peter Street	_____	Green Street	_____	Apple Road	_____
King Street	_____	Brown Avenue	_____	College Street	_____

Look at the bus route on page 73 and check your numbers.

USEFUL INFORMATION: You Want to Get Off the Bus

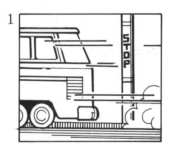

1 Buses do not stop at every bus stop.

2 If you want to get off, pull the cord before you come to the bus stop.

3 Then the bus will stop for you.

4 Sometimes the driver says "Centre doors, please."

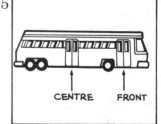

5 That means you exit by the centre doors, not the front doors.

6 You step down to open the doors.

GRAMMAR I: Questions with Does

This is a Yes or No question with **You**.

Do you live on King Street ?

This is a Yes or No question with **He**.

Does he live on King Street ?

This is the answer: Yes or Yes he does; <u>or</u> No or No he doesn't.

3. This is a question with **Ana**.

Does Ana live on King Street ?

4. This is a question with **The 5A bus**.

Does the 5A bus go to King Street ?

5. Make questions.

Does she work on King Street ?

e

Does the bus go to Main Street ?

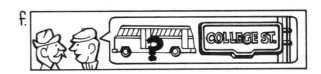
f.

g.

h.

The answers are on page 128.

VOCABULARY: For Listening

PART I: Places

1. school
2. library
3. park
4. hospital
5. post office

6. coffee shop
7. Canada Employment Centre
8. train station
9. bus station

PART II: Directions

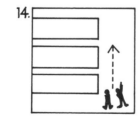 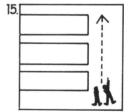  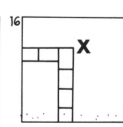

10. Turn right.
11. Turn left.
12. Walk.
13. Walk one block.
14. Walk two blocks.
15. Walk three blocks.
16. It's at the corner.

LISTENING ACTIVITY: Find the Place

a. Before doing this activity look over the Vocabulary on page 76.
b. Put your finger at START.
c. Listen to the teacher's directions and follow with your finger. Where are you?

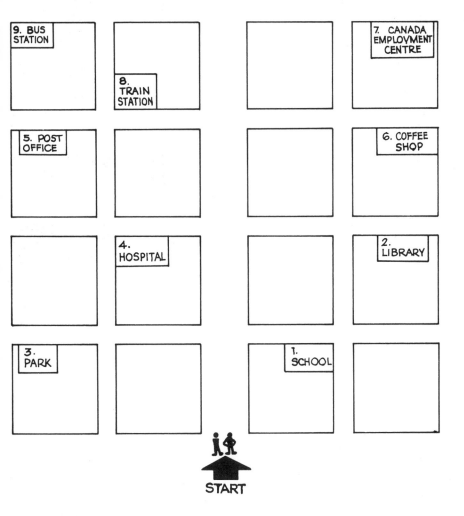

Take a partner.

You are the teacher. Give directions. Choose from these.

Turn right.   Walk one block.
Turn left.   Walk two blocks.
       It's at the corner.

GRAMMAR II: Questions with Where

1 This is a question with **Where** and **You**.

Where do you live ?

2 This is a question with **Where** and **She**.

Where does she live ?

This is the answer: on King Street

3. This is a question with **Where** and **He**.

Where does he live ?

4. This is a question with **Where** and **Ana**.

Where does Ana live ?

5. Make questions with **Where**.

Where does he live ?

_____

Where do you work ?

_____

_____

_____

The answers are on page 128.

78

READING: Bus Signs

Read the signs below. The pictures will help you understand the words.

Cover up the pictures. Look at each sign. Do you understand it?

PRONUNCIATION

These two questions sound almost the same.

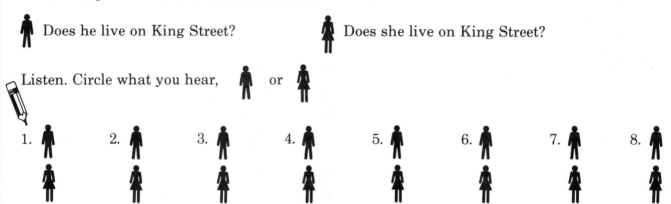

Does he live on King Street?   Does she live on King Street?

Listen. Circle what you hear,   or

| 1. | 2. | 3. | 4. | 5. | 6. | 7. | 8. |

Here are questions and answers about Tony and Ana.

Where does he live? On Simcoe Street.
Where does she live? On King Street.

The two questions sound almost the same. Listen to the question and give the correct answer.

Here are the names of streets you can find in some Ontario cities.
Listen to each name and circle the number of the strong syllable.

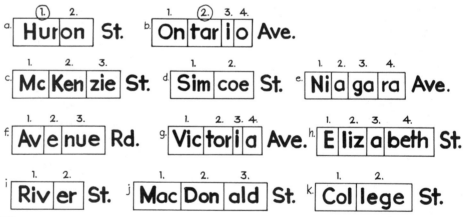

The answers are on **page 128.**

Write the name of the street you live on. _____

Write the name of the street your school is on. _____

Write the name of two or three streets you use when you come to school.

_____

In each street name, show the strongest syllable. Ask your teacher to help you.

EXTRA STUDY: Two-line Dialogues

Complete each dialogue.

1. Why are you tired?
   [C] *I was at the hospital until four last night*
2. Where does Ana live?
   [ ] _____
3. What time is it?
   [ ] _____
4. I'd like an appointment.
   [ ] _____
5. Why are you tired?
   [ ] _____
6. How's your sister?
   [ ] _____

Choose from these sentences.

A. On King Street.
B. How about October 19, at two o'clock?
C. I was at the hospital until four last night.
D. She's fine.
E. I don't know. I don't have my watch.
F. I was at work until twelve last night.

The answers are on page 128.

EXTRA STUDY: Crossword Puzzle
Look in the dictionary if necessary.

Down:
1. Between the front and back.
3. Automobile.
5. Opposite of "right."
6. The number after four.
7. You pull this when you want to get off the bus.
8. Opposite of "back."
12. Please ___ me.
13. The number before ten.
14. The number before two.
15. Short form of "Avenue."

Across:
2. Opposite of "front."
4. The number after nine.
7. Where two streets meet.
9. The number before three.
10. The person who drives the bus is the bus ___.
11. Opposite of "left."
16. A small city.
17. The number after ten.

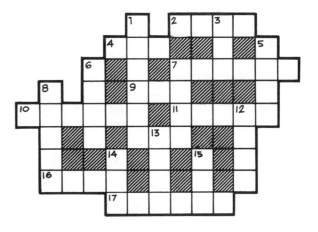

The answers are on page 128.

UNIT 11: GETTING DIRECTIONS INSIDE

CONVERSATION: Lou Asks For Directions

First, look at ALL the pictures. Then look at EACH picture.
WHAT IS THE PERSON SAYING? TRY TO GUESS.

Words for the Conversation on page 84.

EXTENSION WITH CHOICES

Make as many conversations as you can.

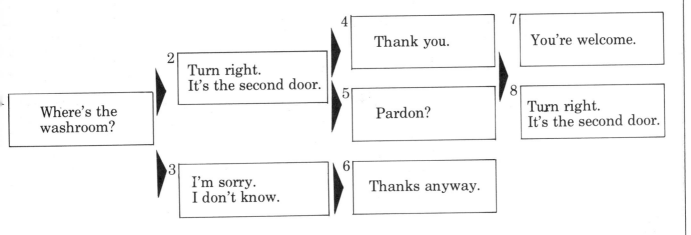

READING: Signs in a Building

Here are some signs that you might see in a building.

Here are the pictures without the signs. Can you remember the signs?

Match the picture to the sign and put the letter in the box.

1. [d] Please use revolving doors. 2. [ ] Fire door. Keep closed. 3. [ ] Caution. Wet floors.

4. [ ] Employees only. 5. [ ] Out of Order. 6. [ ] Wet Paint.

WORDS FOR THE CONVERSATION

1. Excuse me.	4. Turn right.	7. Excuse me.
2. Yes?	5. It's the second door.	8. It's the other way.
3. Where's the washroom?	6. Thanks.	9. Thank you.

Other Sentences You May Hear

Picture 1: Pardon me.
Picture 3: Could you please tell me where the washroom is?
(MORE FORMAL)
Picture 4: It's to the right.
Picture 7: Just a minute. (INFORMAL)
Wait. (INFORMAL)

VOCABULARY: For the Listening Activity

Part I: Places and Objects Inside A Building

1. office
2. exit
3. elevator
4. telephone
5. coffee shop
6. water fountain
7. fire alarm
8. library

PART II: Directions

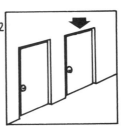

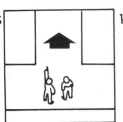
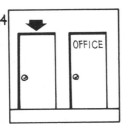

9. Turn right.
10. Turn left.
11. The first door.
12. The second door.
13. Go straight ahead.
14. Next to the office.
15. One floor up.
16. One floor down.

LISTENING ACTIVITY: Find the Place

a. Before doing this activity look over the Vocabulary on page 85.
b. Put your finger at START .
c. Listen to the teacher's directions and follow with your finger. Where are you?

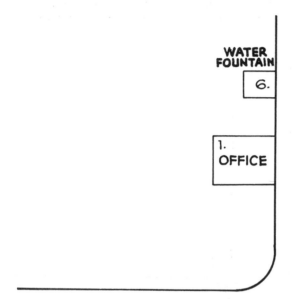
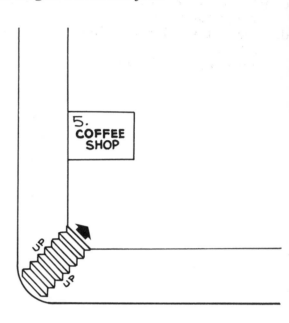
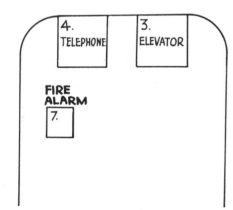

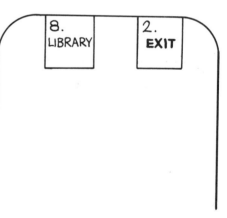

Take a partner.
You are the teacher. Give directions. Choose from these:

Turn right.
Turn left.
Turn left again.
Go straight ahead.

It's

{ the first door.
the second door.
next to the office.
one floor up.

COMMUNICATION ACTIVITY: Directions

a. Tear out each picture card at the bottom of the page.

b. Take a partner.

c. Put one picture card on each star. Your partner doesn't look.

d. Your partner takes one of his/her picture cards and says:
Where's the (exit) please?

e. You look at your floor plan, give directions and your partner puts his/her card in the right place on his/her floor plan.

f. When all the picture cards are placed, check to make sure both floor plans look the same.

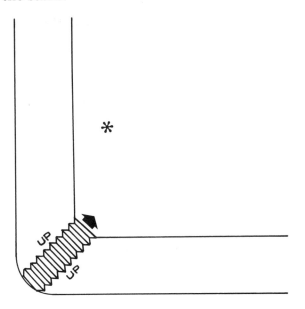

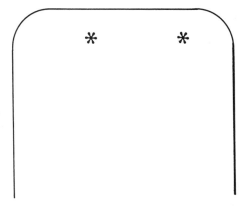

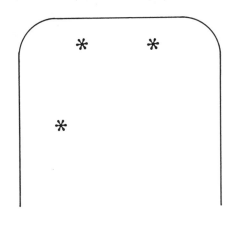

START

VOCABULARY: The Floors of a Building

Here are some doctors' offices in a building.

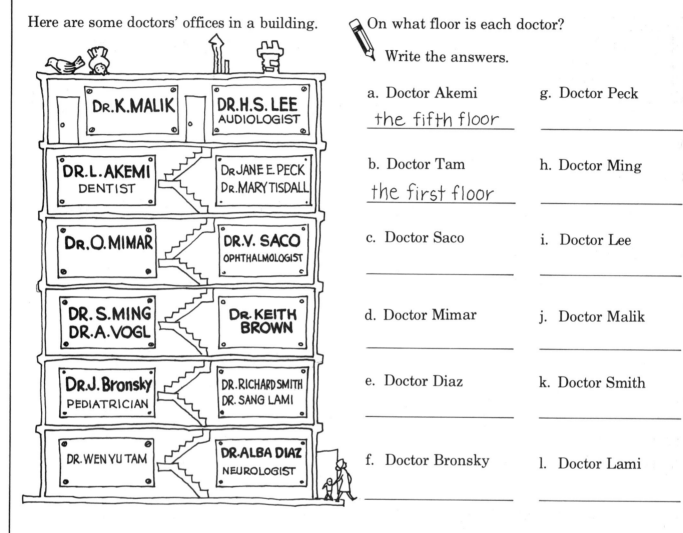

On what floor is each doctor?

Write the answers.

a. Doctor Akemi
   the fifth floor

g. Doctor Peck
   _____

b. Doctor Tam
   the first floor

h. Doctor Ming
   _____

c. Doctor Saco
   _____

i. Doctor Lee
   _____

d. Doctor Mimar
   _____

j. Doctor Malik
   _____

e. Doctor Diaz
   _____

k. Doctor Smith
   _____

f. Doctor Bronsky
   _____

l. Doctor Lami
   _____

The answers are on page 129.

library   fire alarm   water
                           fountain   coffee
                                        shop   telephone   elevator   exit   office

GRAMMAR: Question-word Questions with Is

Long form:

Where | is | the washroom ?

Short form:

Where's | the washroom ?

Where's the washroom?

2. The short form: what happens.

Where is | **Where's** | **Where's** | **=** | **Where's**

3. The short form with **What** and **How**.

What's your name ? | **How's your little boy ?**

4. Make questions with **Where**.

a.

Where's the washroom ?

b.

_____

c.

_____

d.

_____

Make questions with **What**.

e.

What's your name ?

f.

_____

g.

_____

h.

_____

The answers are on page 129.

PRONUNCIATION: The Sound (ə)

A. Look at this word. It has two syllables.

B. The first syllable is strong.
We stress it; we say it louder.
It is called the stressed syllable.

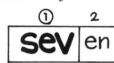

C. Here is the stressed syllable. **sev**

Here is the unstressed syllable. en

D. The vowel **e** in the unstressed syllable is pronounced /ə/.
This weak and short sound /ə/ is called the Schwa.

E. Here are more two-syllable words in which the first syllable
is stressed. The second syllable in each word is unstressed
and has the sound (ə).

1 **quar**ter   The letter **e** is pronounced (ə).

2 **pen**cil   The letter **i** is pronounced (ə).

3 **dol**lar   The letter **a** is pronounced (ə).

4 **làngu**âge   The letter **å** is pronounced (ə).

5 **dòct**ôr   The letter **ŏ** is pronounced (ə).

6 **sec**ond   The letter **o** is pronounced (ə).

F. Here is a two-syllable word in which the second syllable is
stressed. The first syllable is unstressed and has the sound (ə).

7 po**lice**   The letter **o** is pronounced (ə).

G. In most two-syllable nouns in English, the first syllable has the strongest stress.

H. Each word below has the sound (ə). Listen. Which letter is pronounced (ə)? Write the letter.

1. exit   _____i_____   4. nickel _____   7. alȧrm _____   9. welcome _____

2. office _____   5. séntȇnce _____   8. hundred _____   10. about _____

3. July _____   6. answer _____

I. In each word below there is no Schwa (ə). The first syllable has the strongest stress, but both syllables are stressed. There is no unstressed syllable.

11. **cof**fee   13. **Mon**day   15. **coun**try   17. **slow**ly

12. **four**teen   14. **forty**   16. **morn**ing

PRONUNCIATION: Noun Compounds

The words below are called noun compounds. A noun compound is made up of two words. Listen to each compound and circle the number of the strongest syllable.

a.
   ①   2   3

coffee shop

b.
   1   ②   3   4   5

apartment number

c.
   1   2   3

bus station

d.
   1   2   3

train station

e.
   1   2   3

fire alarm

f.
   1   2   3   4

fire department

g.
   1   2   3   4   5

department number

h.
   1   2   3

post office

i.
   1   2   3   4

water fountain

j.
   1   2   3

postal code

k.
   1   2   3   4   5

telephone number

Does the strongest syllable come in the first word or the second word of a noun compound?

The answers are on page 129.

VOCABULARY: For the Conversation

this box

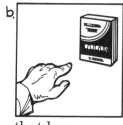
that box

(to) not like

(to) like

CONVERSATION: Lou and Su Ping Go Shopping

First, look at ALL the pictures. Then look at EACH picture.
WHAT IS THE PERSON SAYING? TRY TO GUESS.

Words for the Conversation on page 99.

COMMUNICATION ACTIVITY: The Price of Groceries

Beside **a** write what you pay for each item, or how much you think it costs.

1.  bread
a. _____ a loaf
b. _____ a loaf

2.  milk
a. _____ a litre
b. _____ a litre

3. butter
a. _____ a kilogram
b. _____ a kilogram

4. coffee
a. _____ for 57 grams
b. _____ for 57 grams

5.  teabags
a. _____ for 12
b. _____ for 12

6.  hand soap
a. _____ a bar
b. _____ a bar

7. sugar
a. _____ a kilogram
b. _____ a kilogram

8. toothpaste
a. _____ for 50 ml.
b. _____ for 50 ml.

9.  onions
a. _____ a kilogram
b. _____ a kilogram

10.  potatoes
a. _____ a kilogram
b. _____ a kilogram

11.  beef
a. _____ a kilogram
b. _____ a kilogram

12. chicken
a. _____ a kilogram
b. _____ a kilogram

Take a partner. One of you is A. The other one is B.

A.

Ask what B pays for each item above and write it beside **b.**
You can say:
How much do you pay for (bread)?
or
What do you pay for (bread)?

B.

Answer A. You can say any of these sentences:
$ _____.
I think $ _____.
I don't remember.
I don't buy that.
I haven't bought that for a long time.

USEFUL INFORMATION:
Grocery Products Without Brand Names

Some grocery products are cheaper because they have no brand names and less money is spent on advertising. These products have no pictures on the containers.

Do you buy products without brand names?
Which products?

Brand name

No brand name

READING: Expiry and Packaging Dates

PART I: Expiry Dates

1.
Here is a container of milk.

2.
This is the expiry date. The milk is good until Oct. 8.

3.
On Oct. 7 the milk is still good for use. You can drink it.

4.
After Oct. 8, the milk may not be good.

Today is Aug. 28, 1984. The items below are in your kitchen. Are they still good?

5.
_____Yes_____

6.
_____

7.
_____

8.
_____

9.
_____

10.
_____

11.
_____

12.
_____

Part II: Packaging Dates

13.
This man is packaging meat.

14.
The packaging date is October twenty-first.

Read these packaging dates. Write out each one in your notebook.

15.

16.

17.

SPEAKING ACTIVITY: Directions in the Supermarket

Take a partner. One of you is A. The other one is B. Fold this page in half.

A.

Here are some groceries you are looking for.

bread	coffee
teabags	butter
milk	toothpaste
hand soap	chicken

Ask your partner for directions. You can say:
Where can I find (the bread)?
When you get directions draw in the grocery product.
If you don't know how to draw it, look on page 93.

B.

Give your partner directions. You can say:

▌ **On the bottom shelf.**
▌ **On the top shelf.**
▌ In the next aisle.
▌ In the second aisle.
▌ In the third aisle.
▌ In the fourth aisle.
▌ In the last aisle.

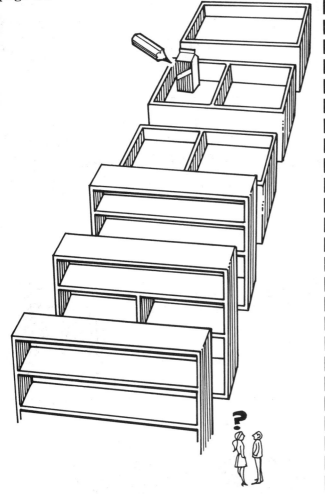

Unfold this page. Check to see that your products are in the correct place.
Then switch with your partner.

1.

This is an
AFFIRMATIVE statement.

| Lou | likes | TRIX | cereal. |

2. This is a
NEGATIVE statement.

| Lou | doesn't | like | MUNCHIES | cereal. |

3. The short form:
what happens.

| does not | does n̸o̸t | doesn̸t | doesn't | = | doesn't |

4. Negative statement with He.

He doesn't like MUNCHIES cereal.

5. Negative statement with She.

She doesn't like TRIX cereal.

6. Make affirmative and negative statements with **like**.

a.

He likes chicken.

b.

He doesn't like beef.

c.

____ ____ ____ ____

d.

____ ____ ____ ____

e.

____ ____ ____

f.

____ ____ ____

g.

____ ____ ____

h.

____ ____ ____ ____

The answers are on page 129.

96

7. Here are two new pronouns.

we

they

8. Here are more negative statements.

I You We They	don't	live on Main St. work on Sunday.
He She Lou Ana My friend	doesn't	have a watch. like chicken. know the time.

9. Make negative statements with the verb **have**.

She doesn't have change.

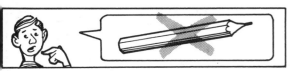

_____

_____

_____

_ _ _ _ _ _ _ _ _

Make negative statements with the verbs **work** and **live**.

f.

I don't work on Saturday.

g.

_ _ _ _ _ _ _ _ _

h.

_ _ _ _ _ _ _ _ _

i.

_ _ _ _ _ _ _ _ _

j.

_ _ _ _ _ _ _ _ _

The answers are on page 129.

97

PRONUNCIATION: The Sounds (ē) and (i).

Meat has the sound (ē). Mitt has the sound (i). The sounds (ē) and (i) can be confused.

1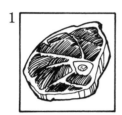

meat

2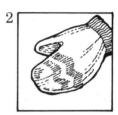

mitt

To make the sound (ē), press the tongue against the upper side teeth and spread the lips.

To make the sound (i), relax the mouth. This is a short vowel.

3

4

Here are more words with the sound (ē), from Units 1 to 12.

5. he
6. coffee
7. seat
8. sorry
9. she
10. thirteen
11. please
12. twenty

Here are more words with the sound (i), from Units 1 to 12.

13. live
14. big
15. milk
16. it's
17. until
18. little
19. chicken
20. six
21. chin

Here are two sentences with (ē) and (i).

a. Do you have the meat?   b. Do you have the mitt?

Listen. Which sentence do you hear, a or b? Write a or b.

22. _____ 23. _____ 24. _____ 25. _____ 26. _____ 27. _____ 28. _____ 29. _____

Here are some other sounds that can be confused.

(e) as in ten and (ā) as in name

(a) as in hat and (o) as in clock

(u) as in look and (ü) as in too

WORDS FOR THE CONVERSATION

1. How much is that?	5. This is a dollar-fifty
2. A dollar-fifty.	for five hundred grams.
3. How many grams is it?	6. But I like this.
4. Four hundred.	7. Okay.

Other Sentences You May Hear

Picture 1: How much does that cost?
What's the price of that?
Picture 3: How many grams does it weigh?
Picture 7: Okay. We'll take this one.
Okay. Let's get this one.

EXTRA STUDY: Crossword Puzzle

Look in the dictionary, if necessary.

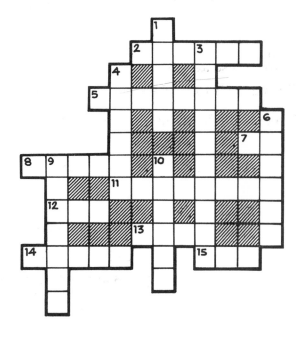

Down:
1. Some people put this in their tea or coffee to make it sweet.
3. We use this to brush our teeth. It comes in a tube.
4. Some people drink this in the morning.
6. After the third and before the fifth.
9. 2 x 50 = one ___
0. After the first and before the third.

Across:
2. We spread this on our bread or toast. It's made from milk.
5. These vegetables have brown skin and grow in the ground. We cook them.
7. Opposite of "Yes."
8. The number after two.
1. This carries you up and down from floor to floor inside a building.
2. This word makes the sentence negative.
3. This part of your body is at the bottom of your leg.
4. Su Ping asked Lou how many ___ the box weighed.
5. Everybody needs to ___ in order to live.

The answers are on page 129.

VOCABULARY: For the Conversation

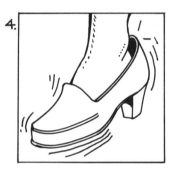

Nouns
1. shoes
2. the size

Adjectives
3. small
4. big
5. a smaller size

Verbs
6. (to) touch

CONVERSATION: Su Ping Goes Shopping for Shoes

First, look at ALL the pictures. Then look at EACH picture.
WHAT IS THE PERSON SAYING? TRY TO GUESS.

Words for the Conversation on page 104.

EXTENSION WITH CHOICES

Make three conversations.

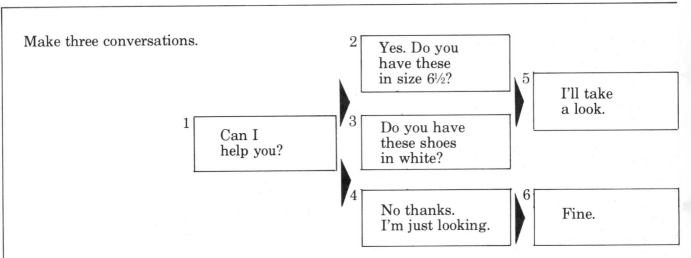

2	Yes. Do you have these in size 6½?
1	Can I help you?
5	I'll take a look.
3	Do you have these shoes in white?
4	No thanks. I'm just looking.
6	Fine.

READING: Instructions for Care of Clothing

Clothing labels sometimes have instructions. The instructions tell you how to wash or clean the clothing. Here are some instructions and some pictures to show the meaning.

a. Dry clean.

b. Machine wash.

c. Lay flat to dry.

d. Low iron.

e. Hand wash.

f. Do not bleach.

g. Line dry or Hang to dry.

h. Use mild soap.

Here are the same pictures. Can you remember the instructions?

Match the picture to the instruction and put the letter in the box.

1 ☐ e Hand wash.

2 ☐ Machine wash.

3 ☐ Dry clean.

4 ☐ Line dry or Hang to dry.

5 ☐ Lay flat to dry.

6 ☐ Low iron.

7 ☐ Do not bleach.

8 ☐ Use mild soap only.

READING: Hours of Business

Before Su Ping went shopping, she called the store to find out the hours of business.

You are the storekeeper. Answer these questions.

1. What time do you open on Monday? ___*Nine – thirty*___

2. What time do you close on Wednesday? ___*Five o'clock*___

3. What time do you open on Saturday? _____

4. What time do you open on Tuesday? _____

5. What time do you close on Friday? _____

6. What time do you open on Thursday? _____

COMMUNICATION ACTIVITY: Hours of Business

Take a partner. One of you is A. The other one is B. Fold this page in half.

A.

You are a shopper. Telephone the store to find out the missing hours of business and write them in. You can say:

What time do you open (on Monday)?
and
What time do you close (on Tuesday)?

Monday	☐ - 6 p.m.
Tuesday	9 a.m. - ☐
Wednesday	9 a.m. - ☐
Thursday	☐ - 9 p.m.
Friday	9 a.m. - 8 p.m.
Saturday	10 a.m. - ☐
Sunday	

B.

You are the salesman. Look here at the hours of business and answer your partner's questions.

Monday	9 a.m. - 6 p.m.
Tuesday	9 a.m. - 6 p.m.
Wednesday	9 a.m. - 6 p.m.
Thursday	9 a.m. - 9 p.m.
Friday	9 a.m. - 8 p.m.
Saturday	10 a.m. - 2 p.m.
Sunday	Closed

Unfold this page. Check to see that you wrote the correct times. Then switch with your partner.

WORDS FOR THE CONVERSATION

1. Can I help you?
2. Yes. Do you have these in size 6½?
3. I'll take a look.
4. Have a seat.
5. Here you are.
6. They're too big.
7. Sorry. I don't have a smaller size.
8. Okay. Thank you.
9. Ken. Don't touch the shoes.

Other Sentences You May Hear

Picture 1: May I help you?
Do you need some help?
Picture 2: Yes. I'd like to try these in size 6½.
Picture 3: I'll see if we have a size 6½.
Picture 6: They're too loose.
They don't fit.
Picture 7: Sorry. I don't have anything smaller.
Sorry. There's nothing smaller.
Sorry. 6½ is the smallest we have.

USEFUL INFORMATION: Returning an Item

When you buy an item, keep the sales receipt.

If you don't like the item,

and you want to return it to the store,

you need the receipt.

In some stores, they will take back the item

and give you a cash refund.

Some stores will not give you a cash refund.

Some stores will exchange the item for something different.

Some stores will give you a credit note, to buy something else.

The credit note is good for a certain time.

When you buy an item, read the sales receipt. It tells about refunds and exchanges.

Usually, if the item is on sale, no refund or exchange is possible.

USEFUL INFORMATION: Winter Clothing

1 It's important to dress warmly in winter. Otherwise parts of your body can freeze.

2 A scarf helps. In extreme cold, you might need a balaclava.

3 Body heat goes out through your head. Wear a hat or hood and cover your ears.

4 Wear clothes that keep body heat in. Wool and down are good materials.

5 Layers of clothing also help keep in body heat,

6 for example: long underwear, tights, and sweaters.

7 Wear boots with a warm lining and/ or one or two pairs of socks.

8 Buy boots that have traction on the bottom so you don't slip on the ice.

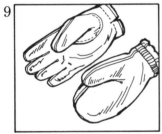

9 Wear gloves or mitts. Mitts are usually warmer than gloves.

10 Look at the labels. Natural materials like cotton and wool are warmer than synthetics.

11 Remember that the cold will affect your body more if there is a wind.

12 For your child you can get a snowsuit. You can attach mitts on a string so they won't get lost.

GRAMMAR AND PRONUNCIATION: Plural Nouns

Don't touch
the shoes.

Singular (one):

shoe

Plural (two or more):

shoes   shoes

2. How to write the plural:

a. We usually add **s** to the singular
   noun.

3. The plural ending **s** is sometimes
   pronounced (z), for example:

a. shoes
b. sweaters
c. pencils
d. gloves
e. bags

5. The plural ending **s** is sometimes
   pronounced (s), for example:

f. caps
g. hats
h. clocks
i. coats

b. If the singular noun ends in **s**, **z**, **ch**
   or **sh**, we add **es**.

4. The plural ending **es** is pronounced
   (iz), for example:

j. watches
k. lunches
l. buses
m. dresses
n. addresses

6. Some nouns have irregular plurals,
   for example:

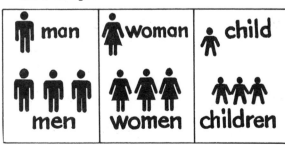

| man | woman | child |
| men | women | children |

Listen. Circle what you hear, a or b.

1. a. ◇ b. ◇◇

2. a. ◇ b. ◇◇

3. a. ✎ b. ✎✎✎

4. a. ⌚ b. ⌚⌚⌚

5. a. 👤 b. 👤👤👤

6. a. 🎩 b. 🎩🎩

7. a. 🥪 b. 🥪🥪

8. a. ☎ b. ☎☎

9. a. 👕 b. 👕👕👕

10. a. 👩 b. 👩👩👩

11. a. 👠 b. 👠👠

12. a. 👗 b. 👗👗👗

13. a. ⏰ b. ⏰⏰⏰

14. a. 🧤 b. 🧤🧤🧤

15. a. 🧍 b. 🧍🧍🧍

Make sentences. Use singular or plural.

a.
Don't touch the shoes.

b. _____

c. _____

d. _____

e. _____

f. _____

g. _____

h. _____

The answers are on page 129.

108

EXTRA STUDY: Spelling

1. Some singular nouns end in a consonant followed by **y**.

   library   factory

2. To make the plural noun, change **y** to **i** and add **es**.

   libraries   factories

3. Write the plural of each noun below in your notebook.

   a. baby   e. lady
   b. fly   f. body
   c. butterfly   g. spy
   d. sky

4. If a vowel precedes the final **y**, keep the **y** and add **s**.

   Singular: day   boy
   Plural: days boys

5. Write the plural of each noun below in your notebook.

   a. key   d. boy
   b. donkey   e. toy
   c. way   f. tray

EXTRA STUDY: Crossword Puzzle

Look in the dictionary, if necessary.

Down:
1. Plural of "woman."
2. Can I ____ you?
4. The feminine pronoun is "she." The masculine pronoun is ____ .
5. Part of the body, below the head.
6. Opposite of "open."
7. The number after nine.
8. Plural of "shoe."
10. The number before twelve.
11. You can carry money in this.
12. The same as no. 6 down.
13. Excuse ____ .

Across:
3. You can wash your clothes in a washing ____ .
6. Plural of "cent."
8. Opposite of "big."
9. Opposite of "yes."
11. Opposite of "front" and part of the body.
13. Plural of "man."
14. Short form of "evening."
15. These keep your hands warm.
16. Short form of "advertisement."
17. You usually need the sales ____ if you want to return an item to the store.

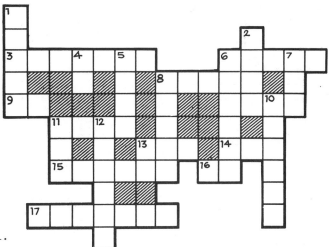

The answers are on page 129.

CONVERSATION: Ana Goes to the Post Office

First, look at ALL the pictures. Then look at EACH picture.
WHAT IS THE PERSON SAYING? TRY TO GUESS.

Words for Conversation on page 116.

EXTENSION WITH CHOICES

Some people collect stamps.

Stamp collecting is a worldwide hobby.

Every year, the Canadian Post Office puts out a souvenir collection of stamps.

Make two conversations:

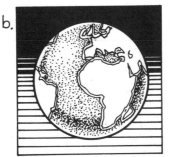

1. Do you have collectors' stamps?

2. Yes. I have the souvenir album for this year.
3. No. I'm sorry we don't.

4. How much is it?

5. Where can I get some?

6. $24.95.

7. You can write to Ottawa. Here's the address.

SPEAKING ACTIVITY

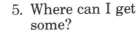
Ask some people in your class these questions:
Do you have time for a hobby? (If yes) what is it?

Write the names and answers in your notebook.

VOCABULARY: Stamps

A. a one-cent stamp
B. a five-cent stamp
C. a ten-cent stamp
D. a twenty-five cent stamp

E. a thirty-two-cent stamp
F. a thirty-seven-cent stamp
G. a sixty-four-cent stamp
H. a one-dollar stamp

Note that there is no **s** on the word **cent**. We don't make it plural.

COMMUNICATION ACTIVITY: Buying Stamps

Take a partner. One of you is A. The other one is B.

A.

Ask your partner for stamps.
You can say:
I need (four 32-cent stamps).

B.

Tell A the cost, for example:
That's ($1.28).

Here are more examples.	
Five 32-cent stamps	$1.60
One 32-cent stamp and one 37-cent stamp	.69
Three 64-cent stamps	1.92
Ten 64-cent stamps	6.40
Two 37-cent stamps	.74

READING AND WRITING: Customs Declaration

Ana sent a package to her parents in Chile. Here is some of the information that she put on the customs declaration form.

1. Name and Address of Sender		2. Name and Address of Addressee			
Ana Pinto 21 Main St. Toronto M6Z 2P2 Ontario Canada		SRA. Gladys de Pinto Avenida Huérfanos 1778 Santiago, Chile			
3. Weight of Parcel	**4. Declared Total Value**				
kg g	$ 51.00				
1 750		**6. Value**		**7. Net Weight**	
5. No. of Items	**Detailed List of Contents**	$	¢	kg	g
1 1	pair shoes blouse	35 16	00 00	1	500 250

8. Sender's Instructions in Case of Non-delivery
a. Unless disposal instructions are given, the parcel will be returned without notice at sender's expense.
b. If delivery of this parcel cannot be effected, dispose of it as checked below:

9 ☑ Return to origin (at sender's expense)   a ☑ by surface
                                                   b ☐ by air

10 ☐ Deliver or redirect to ►   Name and Address
a ☐ by surface
b ☐ by air

11 ☐ Treat the parcel as abandoned

You want to send a package. Fill out this information for yourself.

1. Name and Address of Sender		2. Name and Address of Addressee			
3. Weight of Parcel	**4. Declared Total Value**				
kg g	$				
		6. Value		**7. Net Weight**	
5. No. of Items	**Detailed List of Contents**	$	¢	kg	g

USEFUL INFORMATION: Registered Mail

1. You are sending a package or letter to your friend by mail.

2. You want to be sure that it arrives.

3. You can register it. You can say: "I'd like to register this."

4. You pay money for registration and insurance. Keep the receipt.

5. The mail carrier hands the package to whoever answers the door.

6. That person signs his or her name.

7. If no one is at home,

8. the mail carrier writes out a "Delivery Notice."

9. He leaves it for your friend.

10. Your friend takes it to the post office and gets the package.

11. If your friend doesn't get the package,

12. you take the receipt to the post office and fill out a form to get the insurance money.

Some items can't be sent by registered mail, for example: cash, precious metal or precious stones. If you have any questions, ask at the post office.

GRAMMAR: Yes and No Questions with Is and Are

Statement: **The post office [is] open on Saturday.**
Question: **[Is] the post office open on Saturday?**

Statement: **You [are] tired.**
Question: **[Are] you tired?**

3. How to make questions with the verb **be**. Put the form of the verb **be** in front.

4. Make questions with **Is**.   Make questions with **Are**.

a.

Is he from Toronto?

e.

Are you hurt?

b.

f.

c.

g.

d.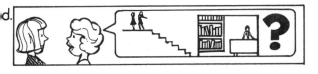

h.

The answers are on page 130.

PRONUNCIATION: Is he vs. He is

1. The voice falls at the end of a statement.

   He's from Toronto.

2. The voice usually rises at the end of a Yes or No question.

   Is he from Toronto?   Yes

3. However, the voice can sometimes fall at the end of a Yes or No question.

   Is he from Toronto?

4. If the voice falls at the end of a Yes or No question, it can sound almost like a statement. Note that in a question, the **h** in the word **he** is often not pronounced. **Is he** is pronounced (izē).

   Statement: He's from Toronto.   Question: Is he from Toronto?
                                                              (izē).

5. Listen. Circle what you hear, a question or a statement.

   1a ?   2a ?   3a ?   4a ?   5a ?   6a ?   7a ?   8a ?
   b .   b .   b .   b .   b .   b .   b .   b .

WORDS FOR THE CONVERSATION

1. Four thirty-two-cent stamps please.
2. That's a dollar twenty-eight.
3. Thank you.
4. How much is this?
5. Two-fifty.
6. Are you open on Saturday?
7. No. I'm sorry. We're not.

Other Sentences You May Hear

Picture 4: How much does this cost to mail?
          How much will this cost to mail?
Picture 6: Is the post office open on Saturday?
          Are you open on Saturdays?

UNIT 15: OCCUPATIONS

VOCABULARY: For the Conversation

musician   instruments   piano   clarinet   painter

CONVERSATION:
Tony and Lou Talk About Their Occupations

First, look at ALL the pictures. Then look at EACH picture.
WHAT IS THE PERSON SAYING? TRY TO GUESS.

Words for the Conversation on page 119.

117

USEFUL INFORMATION: Looking for Good Service

1. If you need a good plumber or mover, ask your friends.

2. If your friends don't know any, there are other things you can do.

3. You can look in the Yellow Pages telephone directory.

4. The services are listed in alphabetical order.*

5. Write down two or three names and telephone numbers.

6. You can call these people and get two or three different prices.

7. You can also ask the Better Business Bureau if a company has had complaints.

8. If someone comes to your door to sell you a service,

9. don't sign anything right away. Take time to think about it.

* If you can't find the service, look in the index. In the Toronto Yellow Pages directory, there are two parts. Each part has a separate index.

In the White Pages directory, there is a section at the back which lists government services. These pages are blue.

READING: The Yellow Pages

Look in your Yellow Pages telephone book. Find these services and write the page numbers.

2.

Opticians . . .
Optometrists, page _____

Dentists, page _____

3. Plumbing, page _____

4. Moving, page _____

5. Television Sales
   and service, pages _____

6. Other _____, page _____

WORDS FOR THE CONVERSATION

1. What kind of work did you do in Portugal?
2. I was a musician.
3. What instruments did you play?

4. Piano and clarinet.
5. What about you?
6. I was a painter in China.

Other Sentences You May Hear

Picture 1: What did you do in Portugal?
            What was your job in Portugal?

SPEAKING ACTIVITY: Occupations

a. Tony's occupation is "musician." Can you say your occupation in English? If not, look in the dictionary or ask your teacher.
b. Ask different people in your class what kind of work they did in their own country. You can say:

Where are you from?
or
What country are you from?
and

What did you do in (Portugal)?
or
What kind of work did you do in (Portugal)?

In your notebook, write the name of each person, their country, and their occupation.

NAME   COUNTRY   OCCUPATION

READING: Advertisements from the Yellow Pages

Read these ads.

Answer these questions.

1. You want to buy a television. Where do you go?
2. Your television is broken. It's 10:00 p.m. Who do you call?
3. You have a Quasar television which is broken.
   a. Who do you call?
   b. What number do you call?
4. It's 7:00 p.m. Your television is broken and you want someone to come to your house to fix it. Who can you call?
5. You want to rent a television set for a period of time. Who do you call?
6. You want your television set fixed by someone who has a certificate from the Ontario Department of Labour. Who do you call?
7. Your television is broken. You want the company with the most experience. Who do you call?

The answers are on page 130.

GRAMMAR AND PRONUNCIATION: The Past Tense

I was a
musician in
Portugal.

What instruments
did you play?
[in Portugal]

I played piano
and clarinet.
[in Portugal]

4. **Was** is a past tense form of the verb **be**. **Played** is the past tense form of the verb **play**.

5. How to form the regular past tense form: add **ed** or **d** to the base form of the verb.

a. Base form: play

Past form:  play ed

b. Base form: live

Past form:  live d

6. Here are some more sentences in the past tense.

Lou

Lou was born in China.
He lived in China until he was 27 years old.
He worked in Peking.

7. Some verbs have irregular past tense forms, for example:

Base form:	go	have	come	eat
Past form:	went	had	came	ate

See page 131 for more examples.

Ana

Ana was born in Chile.
She lived with her mother and father in Chile.
She came to Canada alone.

8. Tell about yourself:

You

I _____
I _____
I _____

9. The plural ending **ed** or **d** is sometimes pronounced (t), for example:

a. help	helped
b. work	worked
c. like	liked
d. walk	walked
e. look	looked
f. touch	touched
g. watch	watched

10. The plural ending **ed** or **d** is sometimes pronounced (**d**) for example:

h. call	called
i. live	lived
j. play	played
k. turn	turned
l. spell	spelled
m. study	studied
n. try	tried

11. The plural ending **ed** is pronounced (id) after **t** or **d** for example:

o. repeat	repeated	q. want	wanted
p. visit	visited	r. need	needed

12. Last night Tony was very busy. What did he do last night?

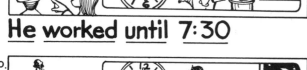

He worked until 7:30

___ ___ ___ ___

___ ___ ___ ___

___ ___ ___ ___

___ ___ ___ ___

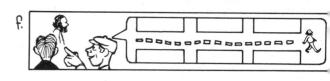

___ ___ ___ ___

___ ___ ___ ___

___ ___ ___ ___

The answers are on page 130.

13. To make past tense questions with all verbs except **be**, put **Did** before the noun or pronoun. Use the base form of the verb.

14. Here are some statements and questions in the past.

a. She ate lunch Did she eat lunch?	Answers: Yes/No. Yes she did/No she didn't.
b. I worked. Did you work?	Yes/No. Yes I did/No I didn't.

15. Make questions in the past tense.

a.

Did he work last night ?

e.

_ _ _ _ _ _ _ _ _ _ _ _

b.

Did they eat at eight o'clock?

f.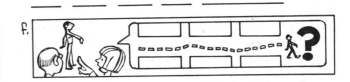

_ _ _ _ _ _ _ _ _ _ _ _

c.

_ _ _ _ _ _ _ _ _ _ _ _

g.

_ _ _ _ _ _ _ _ _ _ _ _

d.

_ _ _ _ _ _ _ _ _ _ _ _

h.

_ _ _ _ _ _ _ _ _ _ _ _

The answers are on page 130.

16. Find out how many people in your class watched television last night, and how many people went to bed after midnight.

123

PRONUNCIATION: Pronouns in Past Tense Questions

1. **Did he** is often pronounced (didē).

> What instruments did he play?
> Did he play the piano?

2. **Did you** is sometimes pronounced (didjü), (didjə), or (didyə).

> What instruments did you play?
> Did you play the clarinet?

3. Listen to each sentence that the teacher says.

Which pronoun do your hear — a, b or c. Write a, b or c.

a.   b.   c.

he   she   you

4. ___   5. ___   6. ___   7. ___   8. ___   9. ___   10. ___   11. ___   12. ___

PRONUNCIATION: The Past vs. The Present

Sometimes the past tense ending is difficult to hear.

now   last night   now   in 1980

13 a.   13 b.   14 a.   14 b.

He looks sick.   He looked sick.   I live on Queen St.   I lived on Queen St.

Listen to each sentence that the teacher says. Which do you hear, a. the present tense, or b. the past tense? Write a or b.

15. _____   16. _____   17. _____   18. _____   19. _____   20. _____   21. _____   22. _____   23. _____

MAP OF CANADA

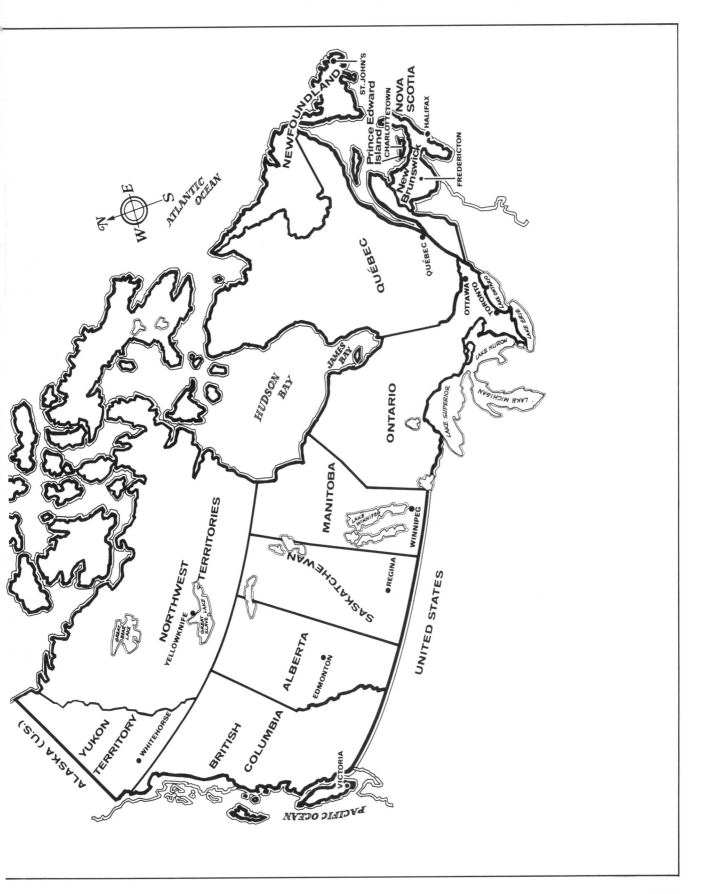

Page 7

29	Chile	17	Lebanon
13	China	23	Netherlands
1	England	26	Northern Ireland
30	France	20	Pakistan
18	Germany	8	Philippines
22	Greece	16	Poland
9	Guyana	7	Portugal
6	Hong Kong	11	Scotland
5	India	12	South Africa
28	Iran	25	Soviet Union
24	Israel	27	Taiwan
10	Italy	19	Trinidad-Tobago
4	Jamaica	2	United States
14	Korea	3	Vietnam
15	Laos	21	Yugoslavia

Page 8

Page 10

2.E   3.D   4.A   5.F   6.B

Page 13

3b. Do you have a dime?
 c. Do you have a nickel?
 d. Do you have a dollar?

Page 19

3d. I work on Queen Street.
 e. Where do you live?
 f. I live on Main Street.
 g. Where do you work?
 h. I work on College Street.

Page 20

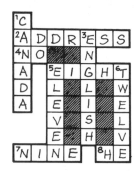

Page 23

Tony: 1. This is Lou.
      2. Lou, this is Ana.
      4. She's in my class.
Ana: 5. Nice to meet you.

Page 25

4b. He's from Sudbury.
 c. She's from Ottawa.
 d. He's from Quebec.
 e. She's from Toronto.
 f. He's from the United States.

Page 26

6c. ① 2   d. 1 ② 3   e. ① 2
 f. ① 2   g. ① 2   h. 1 ② 3
 i. ① 2   j. 1 ② 3   k. 1 ② 3

Page 27

B. grandmother
C. grandfather
D. mother
E. father
G. brother

4A. son
4C. husband
4D. daughter-in-law
4F. grandson
4G. grandson

Page 28

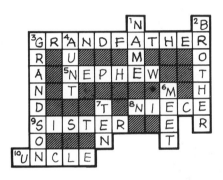

Page 29

.B   3.A   4.E   5.C   6.G   7.F

Page 35

. 1 ② 3   d. ① 2   e. 1 ② 3 4
① 2 3   g. 1 ② 3 4   h. 1 ② 3 4
① 2   j. 1 ② 3   k. ① 2

Page 39

'ony: 1. How's your little boy?
Lou: 3. He's still in the hospital.
'ony: 5. That's too bad.

Page 41

b. I was at work last night.
c. She was at the hospital last night.
d. She was at work last night.
e. He was at work last night.
f. I was at the hospital last night.

Page 43

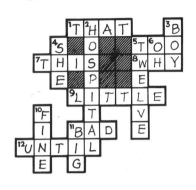

Page 51

4b. I live on King Street.
 c. I have change.
 d. I work on Main Street.
 f. I don't live on King Street.
 g. I don't have change.
 h. I don't work on Main Street.

Page 52

2.b   3.h   4.d   5.c   6.f   7.a   8.g

Page 59

c. ① 2   d. 1   ②   e. ①   2
f. ① 2   g. ①   2   h. 1   ②
i. ① 2   j. ①   2   k. ①   2

ANSWER KEY

Page 60

Here are some possible answers:

2. English
3. Vietnamese
4. English
5. Hindi, Punjabi
6. Chinese
7. Portuguese
8. Tagalog
9. English
10. Italian
11. English
12. Afrikaans, English
13. Chinese
14. Korean
15. Lao

16. Polish
17. Arabic
18. German
19. English
20. Urdu, Punjabi
21. Serbo-Croatian
22. Greek
23. Dutch
24. Hebrew
25. Russian
26. English
27. Chinese
28. Persian
29. Spanish
30. French

Page 67

5c. He works until five-thirty.
 d. She works until six.
 f. He lives on King Street.
 g. He lives on Simcoe Street.
 h. She works on College Street.

Page 70

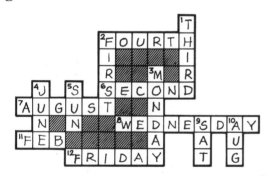

Page 73

3. No   4. Yes   5. 5C   6. 5A   7. No
8. Yes   9. 5B   10. 5C   11. No

Page 75

5b. Does she live on Main Street?
 c. Does he work on Peter Street?
 d. Does he live on Queen Street?
 f. Does the bus go to College Street?
 g. Does the bus go to Queen Street?
 h. Does the bus go to King Street?

Page 78

5c. Where does she live?
 d. Where does he work?
 e. Where does she work?
 f. Where do you live?

Page 80

c. 1 ② 3   d. ① 2   e. 1 ② 3 4
f. ① 2 3   g. 1 ② 3 4   h. 1 ② 3 4
i. ① 2   j. 1 ② 3   k. ① 2

Page 81

2. A   3. E   4. B   5. F   6. D

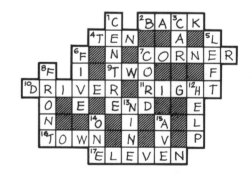

Page 88

c. the fourth floor
d. the fourth floor
e. the first floor
f. the second floor
g. the fifth floor
h. the third floor
i. the sixth floor
j. the sixth floor
k. the second floor
l. the second floor

Page 89

b. Where's the elevator?
c. Where's the coffee-shop?
d. Where's the telephone?
f. What's your address?
g. What's your postal code?
h. What's your telephone number?

Page 91

c. ①2 3   d.①2 3   e. ①2 3
f.①2 3 4   g. 1②3 4   h.①2 3
i.①2 3 4   j. ①2 3   k.①2 3 4 5

Page 96

c. She likes coffee.
d. She doesn't like tea.
e. She likes milk.
f. She doesn't like butter.
g. He likes cereal.
h. He doesn't like bread.

Page 97

b. I don't have a pencil.
c. He doesn't have change.
d. She doesn't have a telephone.
e. I don't have a watch.
g. He doesn't work on King St.
h. She doesn't work on Monday.
i. I don't work on Main St.
j. He doesn't work on Sunday.

Page 99

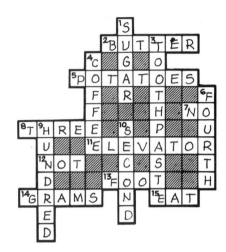

Page 108

b. Don't touch the telephone.
c. Don't touch the dresses.
d. Don't touch the gloves.
e. Don't touch the clock.
f. Don't touch the hats.
g. Don't touch the pencils.
h. Don't touch the coat.

Page 109

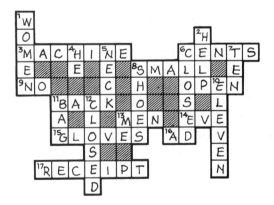

Page 115

4b. Is she tired?
 c. Is the washroom one floor up?
 d. Is the library one floor down?
 f. Are you from Toronto?
 g. Are you tired?
 h. Are you from Ottawa?

Page 120

1. to Main Street TV
2. Brown's Electronics
3. a. Main Street TV
 b. 999-8888
4. Brown's Electronics or
 Main Street TV
5. Main Street TV
6. Brown's Electronics
7. Main Street TV

Page 122

12b. He ate at eight o'clock.
 c. He watched television.
 d. He played the piano.
 e. He played the clarinet.
 f. He walked three blocks.
 g. He visited friends.
 h. He called the hospital.

Page 123

16c. Did she watch television?
 d. Did you play the piano.
 e. Did she play the clarinet?
 f. Did he walk three blocks?
 g. Did they visit friends?
 h. Did you call the hospital?

APPENDIX

IRREGULAR VERBS

SIMPLE FORM	PAST FORM	SIMPLE FORM	PAST FORM
be	was, were	lend	lent
become	became	let	let
begin	began	lie	lay
bite	bit	lose	lost
blow	blew	make	made
break	broke	mean	meant
bring	brought	meet	met
build	built	put	put
burn	burnt (burned)	read	read
buy	bought	rid	rid
catch	caught	ride	rode
choose	chose	run	ran
come	came	say	said
cost	cost	see	saw
cut	cut	sell	sold
do	did	send	sent
draw	drew	set	set
dream	dreamt	shoot	shot
drink	drank	show	showed
drive	drove	sing	sang
eat	ate	sit	sat
fall	fell	sleep	slept
feel	felt	smell	smelt (smelled)
fight	fought	speak	spoke
find	found	spend	spent
fly	flew	spread	spread
forget	forgot	stand	stood
get	got	steal	stole
give	gave	stick	stuck
go	went	swim	swam
grow	grew	take	took
hang	hung	teach	taught
have	had	tear	tore
hear	heard	tell	told
hide	hid	think	thought
hit	hit	throw	threw
hold	held	try	tried
hurt	hurt	understand	understood
keep	kept	wake	woke
know	knew	wear	wore
lead	led	win	won
learn	learnt (learned)	write	wrote
leave	left		

INTRODUCTION TO PART 2

In Part 2 you will find out more about Ana Pinto, Tony Faria, and the Wong family: Lou, Su Ping, Ken and David; and starting in Unit 23, they will be real people in photographs, instead of illustrations. You will also find the language and the activities in Part 2 more challenging.

Here are some of the contents in Part 2:

WELCOME TO
CANADIAN
ENGLISH

A BASIC HANDBOOK
FOR STUDENTS
LIVING IN ONTARIO
PART I

The Ontario Ministry of
Citizenship and Culture